Why and How People Change Health Behaviors

A Collection of Success Stories

Volume 1

By Joseph Leutzinger, Ph.D. and John Harris, M.Ed.

Why and How People Change Health Behaviors

ISBN 978-0-615-21933-2

Printed in the United States of America. First printing 2005.

Published by

HEALTH IMPROVEMENT
SOLUTIONS

Contact information:
Health Improvement Solutions, Inc.
PO Box 241434
Omaha, NE 68124-5434

www.healthimprovementsolutions.com

Quantity purchases of this book are available for educational, business, and community use.

Cover art by Adam Paige

Table of Contents

Dedication

To our families for their continued support.

Joe & John

P.S. — We'll be home soon!

Acknowledgements

This book would not have been possible without assistance from the following individuals:

Wendi Bailey (assisted with finding participants)
Sloane Burke (editorial assistance)
Angie Gall (editorial assistance)
Chris Harter (assisted with finding participants, conducting interviews, and transcribing)
Kane Miller (tremendous help in putting together the final manuscript)
Rebecca Tines (organizational assistance)
Karen Tulley (assisted with finding participants)
Carrin Wiczynski (conducting interviews and research)

We would also like to thank all others, too numerous to mention, who helped us find willing and successful participants, or who provided other forms of assistance.

A special thanks to the individuals who so willingly shared their stories in this book.

Why and How People Change Health Behaviors

Introduction

Why and How People Change Health Behaviors presents stories from individuals who have made successful lifestyle behavior changes and maintained them for a significant period of time. The intention of the book is three-fold: 1) to help those who have not yet made positive behavior changes by providing motivation and insight, 2) to assist those who are currently attempting a lifestyle change, and 3) to serve as a source of hope and support for those who have tried and have experienced failures in the past.

The evidence continues to mount that health behaviors have perhaps the single greatest influence on our health, and thus ultimately our lives. Most people who are not practicing healthy behaviors know they should change, but don't exactly know how. A significant amount of research has been conducted on behavior change theory and various models for behavior change have been developed. These models attempt to account for psychological, social, structural, and other important factors that predict behavior. In spite of this body of work, still nearly 67 percent of American adults are overweight or obese, 60 percent don't exercise, and surprising as it may be, still more than 20 percent smoke. **Why can't we change?**

In trying to answer this rhetorical question, we decided to take off our hats as scientists, researchers, and health promoters, and just ask common people who had made and continued their positive health behavior changes to tell us how they did it. This book tells their stories.

How the Stories were Compiled

We reached out through various channels to find individuals who had made successful lifestyle changes and who had been able to sustain them for some time. People with diverse backgrounds and from various locations around the United States were identified. Originally, written surveys were administered. However, as the surveys were reviewed it became evident they did not capture the whole story, and did not allow the personal elements of each participant's behavior change journey to come through. As a result, the survey was re-structured and administered through a recorded personal interview (see Appendix A for the interview guide). This new approach allowed participants to tell their stories from their own points of view, in a way that is interesting for others to read, and that is motivational and compelling.

Some of the Findings

In this book you will hear from people like Maureen G., who started on her journey by taking one walk with a fellow parent at a little league practice. **(Note that only the initial of the last name of the participants are used in the book to protect their privacy. In some cases the entire name has been changed at their request).** Another story from Tina V. tells how a photo changed her life. People like Larry P. point out inspiration they received from a support group, while others like Gerry R.B., Jose V., and Tim D. made changes by joining programs at their workplaces. E. Dewey S., a 76 year old man who overcame several unhealthy lifestyle habits now enjoys his retirement and looks forward to daily workouts.

As the stories were told some common themes emerged. These were things that many of the participants agreed had worked. The ideas for successfully making behavior changes that the participants told us about included:

• Do what works for you — everyone changes differently.

- Be well informed about the change you are making — Be ready to outsmart the behavior in your efforts to overcome it.
- Be ready — Like anything else, don't go into the effort unprepared or lacking confidence.
- Set goals — Setting measurable goals provides a "yardstick" against which to chart progress and affirms your commitment to achievement.
- Make a total commitment — While different people moved into their changes with differing amounts of speed and energy, all were totally committed on some level when the change finally began to occur.
- Take it one day at a time — Seeing a change as something you are going to have to do for the **rest of your life** is overwhelming. Seeing the change as a series of day-by-day steps makes it easier to accept and comprehend. Most changers expressed that as the days went by, the mental pressures of changing the behavior became easier. In fact, most said their past success resulted in additional confidence and motivation to continue the journey.
- Plan ahead for scenarios that you find threatening — The changers in this book often spoke of the pitfalls they faced. Thinking of what those threatening situations might be in advance, and having a plan to deal with them, helped many of the changers.
- Control your environment — Many changers said that doing things like not going places where temptation could occur, getting rid of the clothes they wore when they were heavier, making their house or office a non-smoking area, or keeping only healthy food in their pantries and refrigerators helped.
- Take small steps — Most changers realized they did not get to their current situations overnight. Thus, they realized that returning to a

more healthy state would take time. For most participants, big changes occurred through a series of small victories.

- Seek support from others — Family members, co-workers, support groups, workplace health promotion programs, and other means of support were all helpful. If you have the support readily available to you, use it! If you do not, find ways to add support to your life.
- Realize that compliments from others are motivating — Many changers mentioned how motivational and energizing compliments were.
- Don't let a short term relapse negatively impact your potential for long term success — Very few of the participants made their changes without some amount of relapse. The difference was that successful changers recognized the mistake that led to relapse, didn't dwell on it, dusted themselves off, and got back on the horse and rode on.
- Know that one successful change leads to another — Success drives success.
- Reward yourself for success — Successful changers took pride in what they accomplished, and gave themselves little rewards along the way. Making one small change, can lead to success.

As you read the book you will find many more tips and ideas. These are but some of the recurring themes.

How You Might Use This Book

There are 44 stories to read, each one equally remarkable in its own way. While reading these stories, if you are someone thinking about a lifestyle change, you may find someone like yourself whom you can model after. Other readers may choose to select good ideas from several stories and mold their own plan. Still others may just need to know it can be done, and use all the stories to help them start experiencing success.

One way to get more out of this book is to ask yourself the questions on the following page as you read each story. You could also use these questions as a guide for discussion with your book club, worksite or community support group, family or friends. While all questions may not apply to each story, we provide this complete listing in the introduction because we have learned that each story can be interpreted differently by each reader.

We want these questions to serve as a source of reflection as you prepare yourself or someone else for successfully changing a behavior. If you want to actually record your reactions to some of the stories as these questions provoke thought, a form on which to do so is presented in Appendix B. Note that if you want to keep this form on your personal computer or your Personal Digital Assistant (PDA), go to **www.healthimprovementsolutions.com**, click on the "Products & Services" link, click Why and How People Change Health Behaviors, and then click on "Behavior Change Planning Log", to download the log presented in Appendix B.

Here are the questions we suggest you ask yourself as you read each story:

How This Story Relates to Me

1. What do I think are the most motivational aspects from this story for me?
2. Can I derive any motivation from this story for my own situation?
3. Do I have some things in common with this changer?
4. What was the most interesting part of this story for me?
5. What was the most surprising part of this story for me?
6. Is this story a good model for me in establishing personal goals?
7. What are my similarities and differences with this changer?

My Key Learning Points

1. What are the key learning points from this story for me?
2. During what part of the story did I feel like the changer finally made the total commitment necessary to make behavior change(s) and what can I learn from this?
3. Do I see the importance of taking small steps that lead to lasting change from this story?
4. Did this story help me put relapse and overcoming it into perspective?
5. Changing two behaviors at once can be too difficult. What did I learn by hearing how this person addressed and successfully changed more than one behavior?
6. Does this story help me understand the importance of rewards?
7. What are the main tips and strategies that I learned from this story?

My Action Steps

1. What was this changers support structure? How will I develop a support structure for making my behavior changes?

2. What did I learn by reading about this person's planning behaviors and what is my plan for change?
3. What environmental changes did this changer make and what environmental changes will I need to make to be successful?
4. What are some small steps I can take now that will help me reach lasting behavior change?
5. How might I reward myself for making a successful behavior change?
6. Am I prepared for relapse and how will I deal with it if it does occur?

The paths to successful behavior change seem to vary as widely as the people whose stories are told in this book. You will read stories from people living all over the country ranging from 23-76 years of age. The stories are told in *their* words. Some chose to tell us a lot while others got right to the point and told their stories quickly. Regardless how the stories were told, there are many lessons to be learned from these successful changers. Wherever you are at, we hope this book creates a launching pad for your successful change.

Keeping the Book in Context

Why and How People Change Health Behaviors is not a research study. While we used health experts to review the concept, the interview guide, and to make recommendations on whom to interview, this book should not be viewed as research or an endorsement of any of the products or programs mentioned in the stories. The mention of specific products or programs simply demonstrates the variety of solutions people have used to help them be successful. So that you know where to find any products and programs mentioned in this book, we have provided contact information for each in the Appendices.

The Role of Personality

Initially, when putting the concept and book together, we wondered what role personality played in making lifestyle behavior changes. As you will see from the interview guide in Appendix A and in the stories, we asked respondents to note the personality type that seemed to fit them best. We sent the interview guide to all respondents prior to the interviews so they could prepare if desired. We also shared a brief description of the personality types. We chose both flattering and unflattering terms to describe the personality types using the Enneagram personality inventory. For more information regarding the Enneagram personality inventory visit: **www.enneagraminstitute.com**.

In the stories you will read responses to personality types and quickly discover that, like their methods, the personality types of the successful changers varied widely. This led us to believe that no specific personality type is required to be successful at making a behavior change. Again, while this book does not provide conclusive research, **it does suggest that people of all ages and genders, representing a variety of personality types, use multiple methods to successfully make behavior changes.**

The Road to Healthy Behavior Change

The road to behavior change is not easily traveled, but it has been successfully navigated by many people. We sincerely hope individuals who read this book become motivated to make positive behavior changes. We would like to identify more of you and learn about why and how you changed. **If you or someone you know is willing to tell us your story, please e-mail us at joe@healthimprovementsolutions.com**. Please put "Why and How…Success Story" in the subject line. We want to hear about the experiences of people old and young (even adolescents), both men and women, from all walks of life, and potentially use your story in our future edition. Your story would be greatly appreciated, and you will be helping others discover why and how to make healthy behavior changes.

We hope you will enjoy this book. If you are someone attempting a behavior change we wish you success and hope this book will serve as a source of inspiration for you.

Maureen G.

37-Year-Old Female
Hartford, CT/Ellington, CT
Weight Loss
Increased Physical Activity
Overcoming Depression

My name is Maureen G. I was born in Hartford, Connecticut the middle child of seven children in an Irish Catholic family. I am 37 year old, single parent, currently living in Ellington, Connecticut.

The behaviors associated with eating were instilled in me very early in life. For example, the food selections we had as children tended to be very bland, and high in starch and sugar. My mother tried to prepare healthy "balanced" meals for us, but by today's standards they really were neither healthy nor balanced. I did not learn about healthy eating until much later in life. Growing up, we were expected to finish everything on our plates. There was an expectation to enjoy what you had that day, because we did not always know what we would be having the next day. I remember sneaking and hiding food as a child. My mother would hide food from us, because my siblings and I would raid the cupboards.

When I started thinking about changing this behavior, there were a number of factors I considered. I was always a bit heavier — I have four sisters and two brothers, and I was always one of the heavier siblings. I had been overweight by 20-30 pounds when I was in my teens and early 20's. In high school, I would avoid taking photographs. I did not want to see what I looked like. Then, as a young, single parent, I experienced years of depression and uncertainty. I focused on anything other than myself. When I was 34, I became very concerned about a variety of things — one being my emotional health. I was unhappy and knew I was not healthy. I couldn't get from my car to my desk at work without becoming winded. I was in denial and not focusing on my health. I devoted time toward raising my son and ensuring I had a good job to support him. Finally, at age 34, I said, "I am unhappy and depressed, and I need to admit it."

My workplace offered various health services designed to assist employees. An employee health newsletter listed the risk factors for diabetes, such as being overweight or having a family history. I recall thinking, "I am a coronary event waiting to happen." I felt like I was one big risk factor. I had purchased various workout videos, but I was so overweight that I physically couldn't use them. I was also one of those foolish people who would begin an exercise program without consulting my doctor.

I began changing my behavior while my son was playing little league baseball, which bored me to tears. I would sit there and think that there had to be a million other things I could be doing. One day as I was starting to fall asleep, one of the other mothers asked if I wanted to go for a walk around the park. During our walk, she told wonderfully humorous stories about herself and her family. She also shared something that made an impression on me. She said, "If you can do something continually for 30 days, you can make or break a habit."

I am a very private person, and I was very self conscious about my weight. Going to a fitness center and being around fitness people was not what I wanted. That is why the idea of walking around my neighborhood was so appealing. I ended up walking each morning before my son awoke. I started out walking 15 minutes, then 20 minutes, and gradually my pace became faster. I became curious as to how far I was going, so I drove my car one day to measure the distance. It was only three-tenths of a mile. I then figured a mile took me 20 minutes to complete. I started thinking, "I can do more than a mile, I can do two miles." I got to the point where I was walking four to six miles a day, and completing a mile in about fifteen minutes. It became addictive. Walking turned out to be the perfect thing for me because it required no equipment. I did find out that good comfortable shoes are very important. Now I always have a back-up pair. At one point I was walking about 15 miles a day. During that time, I would walk in the morning and later in the day when I needed a de-stressor. It has continued to be something that helps to relieve some of the stresses of work and family.

I feel my eating habits changed because of the walking. I began to crave healthier food and shun unhealthy foods.

In 18 months, I ended up losing between 80-90 pounds. I also changed my eating habits. **I feel my eating habits changed because of the walking. I began to crave healthier food and shun unhealthy foods.** I used to eat a whole package of Oreo's in one night. As a child I recalled my mother having to hide food at our house. I still find it challenging to overcome that thinking. The best strategy for me is to eat five-six small meals throughout the day to ensure I am getting a balanced diet. Now I am at the point where I could probably lose about 10 more pounds, but I feel healthy. I modified my diet significantly because I knew it was important if I were to maintain my progress.

Recently I began to change the types of workout routines I do. Sometimes I do Pilates in the morning. If I get bored with something, I try something else for awhile. Right now my routine includes 20 minutes of Pilates in the morning, a walk of four-six miles and Tae-Bo. Other than food changes, I also needed to get a second job to accommodate my changing wardrobe needs. I never used to like buying clothes. Now, when

I want something new I can wear it (laughs). I can now shop at stores where I couldn't shop before!

Barriers — there were barriers, such as watching out for other people's opinions. I found that some people had a negative attitude toward weight loss. People would say things like, "When are you going to stop walking?" I would look at them and respond, "Why would I stop walking?" This is a behavior change in my life and the wonderful side effect is that I lost weight. I also found that it has changed my attitude. I find that I have a sense of humor, and now my general outlook on life is positive.

There has never been a period of more than two days that I haven't walked. I started a group walking club. At work, they had a program called Walking Well. You simply report your walking activity each week. There were incentives and prizes, so I filled out forms and walked three to six miles a day. I received emails from the program coordinators who were in disbelief and asking, "Are you sure you are not sending in too many forms?" My employer featured me in an article in Working Well magazine. In the article, I shared, "Anyone can accomplish this type of success if they want to. But you can't do it for anybody but yourself. You have to want it for yourself."

During my change attempt there were those people who were supportive. My son took such pride in the changes that were happening in my life. I remember one time in particular, I had picked him up from daycare. As we left, he put his arm around me. I thought it was unusual, and he shared that one of his playmates had said to him, "Wow — your mom looks different. She looks like she is losing a lot of weight." He took so much pride in the fact that other kids had noticed.

During my behavior change I did not get help from a health professional.

I did read, but it did not energize me. I think a book — such as this one — that highlights health behavior success stories, would have piqued my interest.

My weight was not an issue, my physician and I discussed. I never felt comfortable or that it was a topic my doctor could help me with. Years ago, an overweight physician made a comment about my weight. I did not feel like it was something he knew anything about or could help me with.

When I think about whether I was prepared for this change, I look back and think that I was clueless. During the first year I may have been walking too much on some days, and damaging my feet and knees; walking to the point where I would get blisters or bruise the bottom of my feet from the constant pounding of walking. I didn't care.

I think I will always stay with this lifestyle change, but it will always be a struggle. I recognize that I have to be vigilant because the ease with which I can go back to poor habits, and allow myself to fall back into my old lifestyle, is very strong. It is a struggle to stay focused. It is work to make yourself happy. It's not something that just gets handed to you — you work for it. It is also not something where you say, "Now that I am here, I have reached my goal and can relax." People say you have to make sacrifices (laughs). I am sacrificing my time, or things that I need to get done. But, if you don't change your health behavior you may also be sacrificing the length of your life.

The advice I would have for others is to do something you truly enjoy, and ensure it is something you can sustain. Whatever you choose to do, especially when it comes to managing your health, it has to be sustainable and not something you can just buy into for the short term. It is something you have to make a part of your life. Also, be sure you are doing it for yourself and not for others. If you do it for yourself, then others will benefit. Take some time for yourself every day. It is so important to find people who can support you. I have a friend who has health difficulties and is very overweight, yet she has been one of my best supporters. She is so happy for me that she told her psychologist that I was her inspiration. I thanked her for mentioning me at the session and then asked her if she could also mention me in a group session (Laughs). Everybody gets to their goals differently. What I did, and continue to do for my health behavior change, is not necessarily what will work for everyone. You need to do what will work best for you — it has to be personal and have a positive impact for your life. **When I awake each morning, I say to myself, "It is time to take care of yourself."**

Larry P.

46-Year-Old Male
Kirkwood, MO
Overcoming Addictive Behaviors
Increased Physical Activity
Weight Loss

I was born, and now live, in Kirkwood, Missouri. I am a 46 year-old, divorced male who completed some college. I have certifications in personal training and weight management.

When my father was alive, he was vice president of manufacturing at McDonald Douglas. My mother worked for the Red Cross before she married my father. My father has passed away and my mother is 83. I believe my parents did the best they could. I think they tried to teach me, to the best of their ability, good morals, concepts, hygiene and all of those things that parents do. There may have been a lack of support as far as direction in my life.

Part of my story is drug abuse, and I think part of that is rebellion towards my parents; the opposite of what they were trying to accomplish. Drinking was certainly acceptable in my family, and alcohol was always present.

My current environment is different than my environment was when living with my parents, and until my sobriety. My previous environment was that of a professional musician, on the road and living that lifestyle. Drugs and alcohol were always present. The difference now is that I have spiritual tools, and I have learned different ways of dealing with issues, examining my life, and looking at things in a more realistic light. So, my current environment is much different. I am no longer around the music scene as much, although getting away from the music scene was not what made the difference. The determining factor was changing my life and getting involved in a support system, a twelve-step program, learning how to live my life, and learning how to live my life without medication. Now, I am a personal trainer, as well as a lifestyle and weight management consultant. I also have a non-profit organization. The primary thing we do is to serve as mentors in the arts with at-risk youth.

It was a hit with (what I like to call) a velvet 4X4. Whenever your behavior becomes out-of-control, there are consequences. I am a big believer in consequences. I am also a big believer in God. I believe that God was trying to draw me into Him, and I think He does that with everybody. He allows circumstances to happen in your life, and when I say velvet 4x4 for example, I have 14 DWI's, but have not been killed; and thank God, neither has anyone else. I have been hurt pretty bad, and have some legal consequences; like short-term jail time. I hit bottom and couldn't go down any further, which was my first spiritual awakening. I reached the point where I thought, "I just can't do this anymore. I can't do this alone, and I need to seek help." So, the catalyst for my behavior change was hitting the bottom. Things in my life kept spiraling downward out of control, until I hit a brick wall.

Oftentimes, when we were out on the road, we would play for weeks. I had this philosophy that there always needed to be sanity along with the insanity. If I was going to go out every night tearing my body down with drugs and alcohol, then in the daytime, I needed to do something to take care of myself. So, I would either workout at the hotel gym, or I would go get a two-week membership at a health club. Other times I would map a running route and try to take care of my body the best I could. I eventually came back to St. Louis with the purpose of getting sober. I had some friends call me that were performing on a cruise ship, and they asked if I would like to become part of their band, as the drummer. So I flew down there, we made a videotape and did promotional stuff. While there, I noticed they had personal trainers aboard this ship, and I thought, "What a cool thing." I could get the education and train people during the day, and play music at night." The gig didn't pan out, but I decided to still go and get the education for personal training. I contacted the American Council on Exercise, which is one of the "gold standard" certification companies in the world, and completed their certification course. I have been personal training for almost six years. I received the certification in 1998. I love my client base, and I am busier than I want to be. I turn away people every week. I train at the Kirkwood family YMCA. I also have gym space that I rent where I bring in private clientele, and I also go to people's homes. Those are what I call my "fitness-to-go" clients. I make myself available for all situations.

I have tackled drugs, alcohol, exercise and diet. The exercise thing, I was kind of doing all along. I was a very overweight child. There may have been some influences from my parents there. When I was very young I had allergies and was really, really, thin, so I think my mother thought she needed to stuff me with food. I may have picked up some bad lifestyle eating habits from that, if you were to go back to the beginning. By the time I came into sobriety, I knew how to eat right. The first thing I knew I needed to do was to get rid of the drugs and alcohol. When I first came into sobriety, I was told, "Do not do too much" (in terms of behavior changes), so it probably took two years after I was in sobriety until I quit smoking.

I quit smoking the same way that I quit using drugs and alcohol. I developed a relationship with my higher power by getting on my knees everyday and asking for the compulsion to be removed. In the end, that is what did it. People can say, "Wow, you have accomplished a lot"; and maybe some things I have accomplished, but certain things I could not have accomplished on my own. Even today, my life is sometimes unmanageable, so I need help to manage my life and that has to come from a source outside of myself.

In regard to exercise, I was not an athlete. I did not like sports, but things changed in my mid twenties. Exercise has been a part of my life, since my 20's. I got sober before I became a personal trainer. Your life has to be your witness. I would say that maybe things became more disciplined, more organized and methodical after I became a personal trainer because I had the cognitive ability to put those things together.

Remember my philosophy? When it comes to diet, during the day I tried to build up my body because I knew I was tearing down my body at night. Except for when I went through my phase of crystal methamphetamine addiction, my diet was pretty good. I had a diet rich in fruits and vegetables, carbohydrates, proteins and fats in the right amounts and proportions. The problem is those other things (drugs) sort of counter-acted that. Of course, when I was addicted to crystal methamphetamine, I was hardly eating anything at all, so I was very thin.

You have to change your play places and your playthings. Your playthings are drugs and alcohol, and your play places are where you go with the people you hang out with to get your playthings. For me, it wasn't that hard because I moved away from California to St. Louis. California was where I was performing most of the time, California and Nevada.

I started to re-structure my whole life. I began going to meetings, and finding a whole new support system. There were new people who became my friends, and I began hanging out with them on a daily basis. I was going to meetings with them and seeing them socially, so everything started to change. In short, I had a lot of social support and a lot of phone numbers of people I could call for support. That is one of the things that happens at meetings, you get a lot of phone numbers, so that if you get the urge to use, you call someone. You are talking to people constantly who have gone before you, so when you have a problem and you share it with

> If you remove the alcohol, but don't remove or work on the other issues, and you don't have the spiritual tools, then you are a dry drunk and are setting yourself up for a relapse.

another, they may be able to share an experience with you, as well as strength and hope that maybe you didn't have before, and that is really how it works. I am a big fan of therapy. I have seen a psychologist on a regular basis. It's about being able to share your emotions, feelings, and what is going on inside you at your core level with someone who can help you.

I have only tried to seriously quit just this one time, and it is working. There were times when people in my band would come to me and say, "Larry, we think you are drinking too much." In fact, it was over a six-year period. I said, "If you think that drinking is a problem, then I'll quit drinking." Which I did successfully without a program, but I didn't change my life. **If you remove the alcohol, but don't remove or work on the other issues, and you don't have the spiritual tools, then you are a dry drunk and are setting yourself up for a relapse.** There were moments of clarity when I would say, "Hey, I need to do something." I would attempt to cut down or quit for a while, but I never thought that I needed to quit or had a desire to quit permanently. It was more like there is a consequence, so I need to do something about this at least for a while. The barriers out there were not allowing me to make the necessary changes in my life. They say, if you keep hanging out in a barbershop, you are probably going to get a haircut.

If you are trying to change your life, and you are new to sobriety, but you are hanging out in bars every day, that is probably not a good idea until you are firm on spiritual ground. One of the things I am a firm believer in, is that once you are on spiritual ground, you should be afraid to go nowhere. If I have a band job, and I have a reason to be there, I shouldn't be afraid to be there. If I am somewhere, and there is a problem, then I need to call a sponsor, or anybody, and possibly go to work with another person. That is the way the program works.

It is very individualized. Here's the other thing, I did go to a treatment center. When I was in recovery, I would speak to my needs. I would say to myself, "This is my way, all my best thinking got me here, all my intelligence, when I thought I was on the ball, it was not happening. I am willing to listen to others and so I worked the program fervently, at least as fervently as I was drinking and drugging. For some people, it may take five years. I got though in about a year. There was one time that I quit drinking for six years. I was still drugging, but I was not in a place at the end of the night when it was time to get paid, were I was passed out in my hotel room. I was maybe doing cocaine or crystal methamphetamine and you are not passed out incapacitated using that kind of drug. It is just the opposite.

This key period was right before I came back to St. Louis. I was an addict, so when I quit for those six years, the last thing that I was really into was crystal methamphetamine. Before that, I would do it with anyone. I would do it until it was gone and then look for more. That is the way that I drank and drugged.

I would never miss a gig. I had never missed a gig in my life, however I did miss one at the end. I was up for five days, and then passed out in a hotel room. Three days later I realized I had missed my first gig. That is when I called my agent and said, "I think I have a drug problem." I called my mother in St. Louis and said, "Mom, I have a drug problem, can I come home?" I still hadn't drank again. That was when I came home and received an evaluation at a treatment center. I hadn't drank in six years, and I then de-toxed myself of the crystal methamphetamine. They said, "We think that you need in-patient treatment, we think that you need to go to a psychologist." And, so I did. I had joined another band then and started drinking again. I only drank for six weeks. During those six weeks, I had a few more DWI's and within a month I was drinking a case of beer and a bottle of acid shots while I was playing the drums.

Here is the way the program works. My sponsor was in, and still is in, a very popular band in the St. Louis area. At the meetings, you see and hear somebody tell their story. They are talking about things like I am talking about, DWI's, going to jail, maybe their family, and not taking care of their kids. Now, they are happy, joyous, and free. You look and listen to that person and want to be like them. That is role modeling. Also, my best friend that lives here in St. Louis is still my best friend today. I would talk to him on a sporadic basis while on the road. He has been in sobriety for 15 years and was telling me, "I was in this program and life is good sober." I don't know if he was a good role model, but he was planting seeds. He is the kind of best friend, that if I didn't see him for ten years and we got together, it was like we were never apart. Before, we may have gone four years without speaking. Now, it is like we are talking everyday.

The exercise certification helped me apply what I was doing in a more correct manner. Now, I specialize more in program design and implementation. I can look at information for somebody and say, "This is your current state of health, and these should be your fitness goals.

A lot is attributable to lifestyle habits; changed lifestyle habits that you can live with for a lifetime. I did learn some more things about healthy lifestyle habits as it applies to physical dimensions of health. The other parts are more spiritual and emotional. **A friend of mine taught me this acronym, it is MEPS. There has to be a balance among these four things: Mental, Emotional, Physical and Spiritual. All of those components are necessary for lifestyle change and balance in your life.** This concept can apply to anybody.

My personal physician was non-existent. I have a physician, but only for a once-a-year physical. I refer a lot of people. It's my job to give referrals. People come to me as an expert to ask for a referral.

I ran a marathon in 1999. I got plantar fasciitis, so I went to a podiatrist. I go to the dentist. I do all of those things to take care of myself, but it's not any one of those things that had anything to do with my sobriety. They were all after my sobriety. I currently run 30-35 miles each week. I didn't use any over-the-counter or prescription medications. There are people that do, which can be the doctor's recommendation.

In terms of being prepared to make these changes, I didn't have any other choice. My choices were real clear, they were right in front of me: death, institutionalization, or some type of recovery. I didn't want to die; I didn't want to go to jail, so I was as ready as I could be. Prepared? Not at all, but ready? Yes. I wouldn't do anything differently if I had to do it again. You are supposed to take this stuff one day at a time, but I do not see drinking and drugging as an option for me in my life.

I would say that I have many of these characteristics in my personality. However, out of all of them, I would have to say "Enthusiast" fits me the best.

My advice to others who want to make behavior changes is to be open and honest, willing and teachable. Be willing to listen to others. If your life is out of control and you are having problems making a behavior change, there is probably something wrong with the way you are trying to do it. Let others in. That is key. Don't try to do it alone.

I think that anyone, not just someone that needs a behavior change, can use solid, spiritual principles in their life. Someone that looks like their life is good, they may have a good job, a nice house, they may have a wife and kids and their kids are in balance, but everyone has their crosses to bear. But in the end, this is the key that I want to get across: Everything in life has a spiritual solution and everybody on this planet can use spiritual principles in their life. If there was one point I want to get across, that would be it.

Tina V. (sic)

Mid-Fifties Female

Midwest

Weight Loss

I live in the Midwest. I am in my mid-fifties. Neither of my parents finished grade school.

I have a stressful job. In the past, to cope with the stress, I would sometimes eat an entire bag of Gummy Bears from 7:00 — 8:00 in the morning. Then, for lunch, I would eat cookies. I had to find a way to stop. I made previous attempts to lose weight and had tried all the diets: Sugar Busters, Macrobiotics, Richard Simmons, Weight Watchers, etc. A few years ago, I celebrated my 25th anniversary with my employer. That same year, my son graduated. I looked at myself in my son's graduation photos and was surprised at how fat my face was. It made me sick, and I didn't want to take pictures ever again. At that time there was a gal in my department who was on Weight Watchers. She would tell me everything she ate that day, the point value, and (if she had a bad day) what she binged on. I thought I would give it a try.

My physician was really happy about my weight loss. I even went below my expected goal, making it down to a size 8. Prior, I was a size 16 petite, which is the largest size carried in stores. I didn't want to become larger because I feared I would not be able to buy clothes.

There is a lady across the street from our house with Multiple Sclerosis. She is a large woman, and we have to go over and help her husband lift her if she falls. Now she has a "Hoya lift" to assist. I don't want to become someone you have to pick-up with an engine lift. I think I would just rather die. It is just awful. When she found out she had MS, she just kept gaining weight, instead of trying to be more mobile.

I lost 48 pounds and kept going. I used Weight Watchers written materials and cookbooks. My support came from people at work, and the Weight Watcher's group.

Once I ran into my mother and sister in a store. My sister had been putting on weight, and made a comment that I looked anorexic. My mother never really paid attention to me, but for the first time in my life, she defended me and said I wasn't going to become anorexic because I knew what I was doing. My mother used to tell me I was fat, so when she stood up for me it made me feel good. When she used to call me fat, it made me want to eat more. When you make a health behavior change, you have to do it for yourself, or you are not going to make it. At one time, my husband told me I was too fat so I pointed out the bad things about him, and since then, he has been quiet about it.

I have always eaten low-fat foods but I am a stress eater. Now I chew sugar-free gum, which keeps me from binging. I do have a mid-morning snack, not because I feel hungry, but for stress relief.

My role model was my friend at work who was in Weight Watchers with me. I was motivated by her attitude and how good she felt. She has a "before and after" picture in her cubicle. She spreads the word.

I don't spend a lot of money on food. Some say they can't do it because they don't have the money. I just buy healthy foods.

I don't think I am going to have any trouble maintaining this change in the future. The program (Weight Watchers) is easy to follow and gave me the tools. So now it is an everyday-thing where I have learned to make better choices. Even when I go out to eat, I make sure that I have enough points left so I can have a treat at the end of the day. My treat is ice cream. If people can find a way to treat themselves, I think they can be successful. If I get off track — I don't fret. **I am allowed to slip every now-and-**

then, as long as it isn't every day. I think if I gain a few pounds, I can just get back on track.

The food available at work is a barrier. I don't even go back and look at the food they offer. I calculate the points out and decide I'd rather eat more than blow it on that stuff.

My personality is the "Reformer". I think I am self-controlled and principled. I am also one of the most rational people in my household right now. I have had bad things happen in my life. Twenty-three years ago, I lost a baby at six weeks to Sudden Infant Death Syndrome (SIDS). I have nerve damage in my ear that affects my balance, which in-turn, limits my driving and exercise. My weight is the only thing in my life that I can control.

I think I could do it alone if I had to, but I prefer to have the support of Weight Watchers and those who are doing the same thing I am doing.

Jason C. (sic)

33-Year-Old Male

St. Louis, MO/Festus, MO

Overcoming Drug Addiction

I was born in St. Louis, Missouri. I now live in Festus, Missouri. I am 33 years-old, married, white male. I went to school through the 11th grade, and have a GED.

Growing up it was my brother, my mom and I. My dad was never around. My mom always had to work, so she pretty much let us raise ourselves. She would go to work in the evenings and come home about 3:00 in the morning. We had the run of the house and did whatever we wanted.

Now, I am married and have two kids. I have a beautiful wife, Kelly C., a daughter and a son. And that's where I am today. My bad behavior began when I started to use drugs and hang around the wrong people. My father was never around because he did not want to be. I started hanging out with the wrong people, and mostly drank and smoked pot. As I got older, I wanted to see my dad. I finally found him and began spending more time with him. My mom told me not to because she already knew his habits. She told me how he was, but I wanted to see him anyway. I started hanging out with him and the next thing I knew he started pulling me down with the harder drugs, womanizing, and everything like that. I started taking on his bad habits. My marriage started falling apart, and my wife was about to leave me. I started exercising to get my head straight.

You always think about changing your ways, so I was always thinking about changing as I was doing the wrong things. I found that when I got around my dad, I started messing around with the wrong stuff. During this time I was married and my wife stuck by me as long as she could. But, eventually she just couldn't take it anymore. After about nine months of going to church, exercising and staying on the right path, she saw that I was serious and she came back. **We were about two weeks from going to court for our divorce and she just dropped it and we've been back ever since. My wife and children helped me change my ways. I want to be able to do things with them as a father. I want them to be proud of me.**

The high I get from exercise saved me from the drugs and loss of my marriage. I'd rather feel good naturally than feel good with chemicals. My mom was, and still is, very health conscious. She used to model and has always taken care of herself. She influenced me growing up. I think it is important to take that into consideration even when you stray from the path. You always come back to the foundation on which you were raised.

My dad used to exercise before he got into drugs. My mom told me that he was always in shape and well built. That always impressed me, even before I reconnected with him. I wanted to be like my dad until I reconnected with him, and then I was disappointed.

I wanted to change when I first had my daughter, but I didn't. I wanted to change when I had my son, and I didn't. What really put me over the top was when I failed my drug test at work. My wife found out about it and wanted to leave me. She also found out that I had been lying to her all this time about drugs and that I'd been messing around. My employer sent me to rehab to give me a chance. While there, I started realizing the bad shape I was in. They were checking and monitoring my blood pressure. I didn't realize the importance of my health because of the chemicals I was taking.

Right now, I'm a truck driver. When I first started driving it was stressful. I ate for comfort and because of boredom, and I gained 50 pounds.

My blood pressure and cholesterol were high, plus on my days off, I was doing drugs. I never did drugs while I was working. Also, when I was doing drugs, I would not eat for two or three days because I was taking amphetamines. However, when you come down you are eating everything in sight and you pack the weight on. Your body has been starving for two or three days and when it does get food, it stores it. When it stores it you just gain weight.

I always had a desire to be in better physical shape. It was something that made me feel good. I have always been built well, just naturally, but I let it go. The drugs were really harmful and they were really affecting my health. For example, my blood pressure was out of control. You feel great when you first start working out. You feel renewed and healthy. Then you start feeling like you are doing it for nothing. You don't see results like you did when you first started. You start to wonder, "What am I doing this for?" And "Is it really helping?" You know, you start reflecting back on your old ways but you just keep on going. It takes a little bit of time, but you are making progress as long as you stay with it. Exercise and quitting drugs has helped me change other health areas. For example, my cholesterol is lowering, I have lost weight, I have more muscle, and my attitude is better. Working out relaxes me and gets rid of a lot of stress.

I started off watching what I ate. I also found things to do with my time. I kept busy. Even though I would not feel like working out some days, I would go and do a half pace workout, just to do something. Before you know it, you've completed a good workout. Also, you get a good feeling when you workout. It motivates you, that thing you get from feeling good.

Today, family serves as my support structure by telling me how good I am and how good I look. Other people giving me nice compliments at the gym and saying they can see the results is also supportive. They helped me with my workouts by answering my questions.

I don't work out when I am on the road. I workout when I am home for three days, everyday, and then when I am on the road I do nothing but eat right and let my body recover. When I workout I lift chest and biceps the first day. The second day I do shoulders and back, and the third day I work legs and triceps. I work abs every day. I also run 30 to 40 minutes on the treadmill each day. I watch what I eat when I go out and I bring my food with me when I am on the road. It is very important to take healthy meals to work. I take a duffel bag of healthy food with me for the week. As a family we go to buffets. My kids still eat all that stuff and can eat a lot. My wife is pretty health conscious, but she likes to eat too. I'll watch what I eat but I am going to let them enjoy themselves.

In regard to relapsing, I went back to using drugs for a week. I was off of them for about a year, I relapsed because I went back to one of my old friends. Once you are off of drugs for that long you realize that you don't miss it. It wasn't as good as before. That was a wake-up call for me. I also relapsed on working out. There were times I would go for two weeks without working out. The good feeling comes back as soon as you start working out again. You feel good and it motivates you.

In the beginning, I would work out for a couple of weeks or maybe a month and then I wouldn't exercise for six months to a year. I did this kind of schedule four or five times before I finally was able to stay with it. Sometimes you can get too serious with it and not enjoy yourself. Making it as enjoyable as you can is very important. You have got to make it fun. If you make it seem like work, you are not going to enjoy it and you will relapse because you work enough already. Why would we want to exercise on our days off and not have any fun? Magazines influenced me. I did not have a role model. I would read muscle and fitness type magazines. I also used the Internet. Going to church really grounded me big time, too. That is always a good foundation. Having

Jesus in your life. I want to be the father that I never had to my children. I want to be healthy as they grow up, and I want to better myself. I just want to be a better person. I have been working out consistently for a little over a year and the results they've seen have been tremendous. I constantly have people coming up to me asking me "How do you do it? Can I ask you questions about working out?" That makes me feel good.

I saw a therapist for a year to help me get off the drugs. I saw him twice a month and then went down to once a month, after three months. Then I saw him once every six months. "What are you doing? Is everything working out? Do you have any questions?" he would ask. Generally, you are on your own with your behavior change, but they are there if you have questions. They guide you in the right direction. I did counseling along with books and magazines. I would also ask others a lot of questions at the gym.

I had anxiety when I was 18 or 19. I went to the hospital with severe anxiety attacks. I couldn't control them. My heartbeat was like 230 beats a minute while lying on the table. The doctor said "You'll be on medication for the rest of your life." I said "No, I won't." I asked what else I could do. He told me that I needed to release some stress somehow. I didn't take his advice until a couple years ago, although I was never on any medication. Originally, I tried to relieve stress by doing things that were illegal, which worked for a while, but they were tearing me up in other ways.

In terms of being prepared for this change, I would say you are never totally prepared. You may think that you are or hope you are, but really you are never totally prepared. So always be aware that you are not going to be fully prepared. But that's part of the excitement. You are going to learn something going through the process. You are going to learn things and that makes it interesting. Who wants to go into something that they already know everything about? That's no fun. What better time to start than today. Have fun with it.

If I were to do it all over again, I would start earlier. Way earlier! I could be way ahead of where I am now. You know the kind of damage you've done to your body, but everyday that you wait you are doing more, even though you may not see it. That's the scary thing, you don't know what's going on inside.

Regarding being able to maintain this change in the future, I have heard the first year is the hardest time. They say if you can last that first year, you've got it whipped. That first year is really tough. So, I've made it past that and I feel great.

Now I have changed my personality. Now I am the way I should have been all along because drugs alter your personality. I believe I am a "Loyalist". When I was on drugs, I thought I was the "Achiever".

The advice that I have for others is to start today because tomorrow may be too late. Also, don't make it feel like work, make it fun and try new things. Other advice I have is don't do the same workout all the time, you'll get bored and your body won't respond either. Remember, your body gets used to the same workout. Also, mix it up, make it fun because you are trying new things. **If you fall off the wagon, don't worry, get right back on. Look at the future. Look where you want to be a in a year. Set goals. Conquer them and then set new goals.**

I have been through a lot in my 33 years of life; a lot of personal things that I haven't even mentioned in this interview. And I rose up from where I was. If I can, anybody can. **You have got to make the change for yourself and then you and others will benefit. But do it for you!**

Judy W.

56-Year-Old Female

Tarkio, MO/Hermiston, OR

Quit Smoking

I was born in Tarkeal, Missouri. I now live in Aregen, Oregon. I am 56 years-old, married, and have two associate degrees. One degree is in business the other in nursing.

I had a very religious upbringing. My parents did not smoke, so smoking was frowned upon in our household. It was a rebellious act when I started smoking at 19. At that time, I was just trying it out. I did not smoke regularly until I was 25, which was another rebellion. I had found out that my ex-husband was chewing tobacco, which I thought was a filthy habit. He hated women smoking — so I started. I had tried to quit through the years, and would refrain from smoking until something stressful would happen. I quit in 1987, and did not smoke again until 1994. In 1994, I lost my daughter in a car accident and, to cope with that tragedy, I started smoking again. After that, the notion of quitting was much harder. I wasn't in the frame of mind to quit again. My husband had stage II emphysema, so we did not smoke inside the house. I was constantly smoking on the sly, but everybody knew I smoked. I never did smoke around him. I didn't smoke in our cars either. I would smoke at work, or when out with my friends. After he was diagnosed with emphysema, he stopped smoking immediately. **Being a nurse, I knew the effects of second-hand smoke. But, I never thought of second-hand smoke clinging to my clothes and being just as detrimental to his health as smoking in front of him, until I researched second-hand smoke for a presentation I gave for the safety group at work.** I became conscious of the danger I was placing, not only on my husband, but on my grandchildren, and any other non-smoker I was around.

That is when I decided to quit smoking. I quit smoking "cold turkey" on May 21st of 2004. Unfortunately, I cannot take smoking cessation aids or medications due to my allergies.

When the state of Oregon prohibited smoking in the workplace, it seemed to decrease the amount of people smoking, but it didn't dissuade me from smoking. When I was placed in charge of the smoking cessation program, as part of my job, it made me feel guilty. I was constantly teased by other workers who would say, "Hey you teach us not to smoke, but yet you smoke!" I would respond, "That only proves that I'm human," or "Do as I say, not as I do." But, I had guilty feelings. We have tried to have a smoke-free campus here at work, but can't get two other departments (that have too many managers who smoke) to go along with us.

I do feel like I went through stages during my attempts to quit. The first phase would be a very strong feeling of, "I'm not going to smoke." Then I went through a phase of wanting to smoke; the desire would be back. I'd restrict myself from being around things that would make this urge stronger. The third stage was "One wouldn't hurt." All it took was that one cigarette and I was right back where I started. This last time I didn't have any of the urges. I think I had a better mindset. I just seemed to be ready to quit. I can't really make it any clearer than that.

For support, some of my co-workers were very helpful. This time, they didn't pressure me to join them for a smoke break. Here, it's a very social thing. Everyone goes out to the designated area and stands around, chitchats, and smokes. Many of them said, "We are proud of the fact that you're not smoking and we wish we could stop smoking." Now, I go on break with them when they smoke, but I stand uphill since the smoke now makes me sick. I throw in my two cents worth, and a couple of people are almost ready to quit — so hopefully I will influence them.

Because I didn't smoke at home, or in the car, I didn't have to make any changes there. At work I had to stay away from the smoking area when I first stopped smoking. I had to stay away from that familiar area until I felt I was strong enough to visit without it bothering me.

Previously, my biggest barrier that prevented me from quitting was friends that would loan me cigarettes. Instead of them saying, "No, you quit smoking" — it would be an automatic reply of, "Well, here have a cigarette." And, I wasn't strong enough to turn it down. I would also be in social situations where smoking was a part of the event. That's the one thing you can't do when you first quit smoking, be in situations where you will want to smoke. You need to make sure you're in a non-smoking section in a restaurant, and not around people that smoke. Now I can socialize with smokers, but it took me about a month to be able to. I do have to be careful around somebody that first lights up a cigarette. That acts as a trigger for me. I have a mindset now that I didn't have in the past. **Before, I would let triggers lead me back to smoking. I have a mindset now that I will not allow this, and that I'm stronger than the cigarette.**

I'm also working on another behavior change that I hope to accomplish, and that is weight loss. I have helped friends. My father had a massive heart attack. He's a diabetic and is on a very restrictive diet. I've been working with he and my mom. He has lost 10 pounds and she has lost six. I have to say that I am my own worst enemy; I only eat once a day, which has greatly lowered my metabolism. So, weight loss is going to be my next challenge. We are all constantly making lifestyle changes.

My stepfather was my role model for quitting smoking. Before he and my mother met and married, he smoked. He'd often tell us how hard it was to quit, and he still says that certain things trigger his desire for a cigarette. He hasn't smoked in 50 years, but shared that it is like any other disease or addiction.

My main motivation for quitting was my conscience. Smoking is now frowned upon by society. Also, being a nurse I feel like I'm lying in projecting healthy attitudes and life style changes when I am not being healthy.

A behavior change cannot be done overnight. There will be dips and hills, but it can be done.

The knowledge for the change came from all the smoking cessation programs I've conducted. I used the Internet to research second-hand smoke. My physician was also very supportive. He'd ask, "Are you still smoking?" I would feel like a red flag was waving. When I did quit, he asked me to come in every three months instead of every six. I have asthma, and he informed me that when I quit smoking I might have increased symptoms. At first I did. I had a terrible time with my asthma and my allergies. I've had to increase my medication, and he's increased his monitoring of my asthma.

The other times I tried to quit, I wasn't as prepared as I thought. I realize that I was much more prepared psychologically this time. I had a much greater desire to quit this time.

To others I would say — If you don't succeed, try it again, because there will come a time when you will do it. I think that I would have quit earlier if I would have known what I know now, including how to handle stressful times when making a lifestyle change. I didn't know how to do that then, so when I lost my daughter, I fell back on my crutch. It was comfortable. When my father had his massive heart attack, I immediately realized it was a bad time, and that I was at risk for smoking again. That's when I started the oral comfort of sucking on a toothpick or sucking on a mint, and making sure I didn't keep company with smokers. I reminded myself of why I quit smoking, and told myself that I was stronger than cigarettes.

If I had to do it again, I would do it earlier. I don't think that I will have trouble maintaining the change in the future. I have a different mindset than in the past, and I recognize that now. Every year I have learned information that helps me. Now I must sit and write my experiences out, and apply it to weight loss. I think I'll successfully change my next behavior.

I have the "Challenger" personality. My advice to others that may want to make a lifestyle change is that you've got to have the mindset first. You've got to want to do it if you are going to be able to do it. You can't do it for anyone else, you have to make the change for yourself. I think that is the greatest thing of all. Today is the first day of the rest of your life. If you're strong enough, you can get it done. **A behavior change cannot be done overnight. There will be dips and hills, but it can be done.**

Gerry R.B.

59-Year-Old Male

New England, ND/Jacksonville, AR

Quit Smoking

I was born in New England, North Dakota and now live in Jacksonville, Arkansas. I am 59 years-old, married and have a high school education.

I started smoking right out of high school, and smoked until August 12, 2002. I was in athletics, so I really don't know why I even started. I didn't hang around anyone that smoked. Both of my parents smoked. In the later years, they both quit and I was still smoking. I really don't know if they had an influence on why I smoked or not. I have one brother and two sisters, and they all smoke. My sister has emphysema and has to be on oxygen. It was always on my mind to quit, but I just never did. I think about it a lot, and I still just don't know why I started.

It was really easy to smoke at work, so I am sure my environment influenced me. It made it hard when they said "no smoking" in the workplace. You would go outside and freeze to death smoking, all the while wondering why you did it, but still never quit. I still smoked as much, because I would go out there and smoke two or three to make up for not being able to smoke inside. All the guys out there smoking would always talk about quitting. As a matter-of-fact about all we talked about was how smoking is such a bad, dirty, stinky habit.

My wife and I were both smokers. She quit 20 years ago. I stopped smoking in the house to please her, but I never quit all together. My wife and kids were always telling me I needed to quit, so I feel like she and the kids were the biggest influence on why I quit.

Over the last 20 years I thought about quitting. I tried so many times. I would quit for a day, for a 1/2 hour, or for a couple of hours. It would maybe last a couple days, but I would always go back to smoking. I tried Zyban, patches, the works, over the years, but none of that worked for me. I have heard other people say it helped them, but not me. Maybe it does help other people, but for me I just had to make up my mind to quit and that was it, that's all I had to do. I tried so many times, but I finally just decided that I wanted to do it.

In my younger years, it was easy to smoke and drink at the same time. Once I quit drinking, I smoked less. It was a bad habit. I smoked at work and at home. I stopped smoking in the house for my wife, but I always smoked in the office. I would always have a cigarette burning in the ashtray. I wouldn't necessarily smoke all day, but there was always one burning.

I guess it was a little bit of everything that made me quit. At the workplace people pushed the smoking cessation programs and stuff. But all I had to do was put it in my mind why I wanted to quit and I did. Everyone on the railroad (the place where the interviewee works) smokes and always talks about quitting, so I guess it was a social thing as well.

I do feel so much better since I quit. I suppose I have gained weight, and I would like to start exercising. They say that when you quit smoking, food will taste better. You feel really good all the time.

Quitting drinking wasn't a huge problem, but smoking was terribly hard. I tried to quit so many times in small increments. I would always say that I was quitting, but then I never did. Like I said, I would quit for an hour or a half-a-day or a couple of days, but always would go back. It was really hard to quit, really different, but a good feeling. I had the control and it was a great feeling because I was making the decision myself. That was major. I didn't use anything to help me.

There were four or five guys here at work that decided to quit too and we all supported each other. At that time I just smoked at work, so the fact that they were trying to quit too, made it easier. It was nice to have peers to do this with. We talked about it and patted each other on the back a lot. We were honest with each other about when we slipped and would have a cigarette or two, but they were always very supportive. Also, no one was about to back out of the deal, so it made it easier. We would all say, "How are you doing? Oh, I have had one or two." But they would always pat me on the back and they would say, "I wish I could be that way — I wish I could quit like that."

After I quit I would still go outside and talk to all the guys out there smoking. The smoke didn't bother me too much. I just wanted to encourage them to quit and tell them how much better they would feel. Once I quit, I knew I was never going to go back, so it wasn't hard to go out there and talk to the guys about it.

My wife and kids were supportive and my sister has been too. Quitting with co-workers was also good. Mainly everyone was reinforcement. My co-workers telling me that I was doing a good job and that they were proud of me was good reinforcement. All the smokers would pat you on the back. They, more than anyone I guess, were my biggest supporters because they knew exactly how hard it was to quit. They wanted to do it themselves, so they were all real proud of me and made me feel real good. They were a big source of support. The doctor would always tell me he could get Zyban or get me some prescription samples for me. He preached a little bit, every time I saw him. I would just put it out of my mind because I knew what he was going to say.

It was nice to go to the doctor and tell him I wasn't a smoker anymore. I would go to the doctor and he would ask if I was a smoker and I would say "yes," and then he would just tell me that I needed to quit. So it was really nice being able to tell him that I quit. It was great not to get the same old lecture about quitting.

Changes at home were big because I couldn't smoke there due to my wife. I used to smoke in my car. I didn't in my wife's car though, so that was real different. I tell people that they can smoke in my car if they want, because that doesn't bother me. It was also real nice to go into restaurants and say that I wanted to sit in the non-smoking section.

I left work one evening about a week after I quit. It really hadn't been that hard of a day or anything, but I stopped at a gas station two blocks away from work and bought a pack of cigarettes. I got in the car and lit up, and then thought to myself — what am I doing? I threw them all out the window and that's the only hard time or problem that I can remember having. All I kept thinking was that I just threw $3.50 out the window! I just realized how stupid I was being, made up my mind and threw them out.

I don't know how many times I tried to quit before I was successful — probably 50 to 60 times. They were all little attempts, like an hour or a day. I don't know if it counts, but I know I thought about quitting an awful lot and tried a lot. There were many times where I said that I did, but I really didn't.

I stopped drinking 30 years ago. I started drinking the same time I started smoking — right out of high school. I guess the reason I stopped drinking was because my wife quit and became a Christian. I saw the positive influence it had on her and that made me want to be better. I would see her going to church and I was going to the tavern and I didn't feel good about that. She made me want to change. We found the good Lord and that made me want to be a better person.

My role models were my wife because she did it, then probably my sister. My wife quit and I saw how it affected her. She would talk to me about it, not pushing me or anything, but just talking about it. She was my greatest role model. The good Lord finally convinced me to change. I think that is the biggest thing. The good Lord helped me.

If I had to do it over, hopefully I would do it a little sooner or not smoke at all in the first place. I don't think I will have trouble refraining from smoking in the future. I sure hope not. I really don't know why I would.

I think that the "Peacemaker" personality type describes me best. I think that it hindered me as far as making up my mind, and following others was something easy to do. I had to take an approach different than my usual one in order to succeed. And, I procrastinated, so I really think that all this hindered me.

What advice would I have for others who want to stop smoking? Just quit! I don't know how, but they just need to do it. They will be so happy they did. They just need to make up their mind and do it. Whatever it takes, and whatever they need to do, just make up their mind and do it. **Everyone's got a different way, so just find that way and do it, because you will feel so much better than you do now.**

Rhonda G. (sic)

27-Year-Old Female

Greenville, SC/Debary, FL

Weight Loss

I was born in Greenville, South Carolina. I now live in Debary, Florida. I am 27 years-old, single and female. I have an Associate's of Science degree and am currently working on my Bachelor's degree.

My mother was a single mom and worked full-time, so she was very busy. She was also into organic foods and was a partial vegetarian, so she didn't eat red meat. Nutrition-wise, I had a well-balanced upbringing. The only thing that had a negative effect on me was that she was quite strict about sodas, junk food and that kind of stuff. So any time I could get my hands on junk food, it was a big deal.

My family, in general, is large built. I have three sisters and we're all six feet tall. None of us are particularly petite. I didn't start gaining weight until mid-high school. I quit getting taller but kept getting bigger. I continued to eat instead of slowing down as I stopped growing.

One day, I had one of those moments. Sometimes people struggle with a starting point, but I literally had an exact moment when something happened that made me change. It was my sister's eighteenth birthday party. I was 22. We were sitting at the table and I was trying to get comfortable when I realized that I could no longer cross my legs because they were, literally, getting so big. I thought, "Okay, this is kind of creepy." Then as the night went on, we were all laughing, and I realized that I could see my own face — my cheeks and my eyes — my face was getting so pudgy. I thought, "Okay, this is ridiculous. Now my mobility is becoming affected." It wasn't really about, "Oh, I want to look good in a bikini," it was more about my health. I was getting to the point where I was going down a very bad path. So at that moment, I thought, "This is it. I have to do something about this." That was the moment I decided to change my behavior.

My mom raised us to always confront things, so it wasn't that everyone ignored the fact that I was overweight. We were always taught to tackle things head on and say, "This is a problem, how can I fix it?" Being able to problem solve made a big difference in being able to break my health behavior change down into smaller pieces that made it a doable change.

I'm a retail manager at Home Depot, which can be kind of stressful. However, I've learned to leave the stress at work. It doesn't really affect me. My family has always been very active. We don't sit around and watch TV; we canoe, go for walks, or bike rides, so I've always been around active people, which has helped. I try to surround myself with activity all the time.

There were stages in losing the weight. I experienced emotional and mental stages. To get a little perspective, I am 5'8" and the highest weight I can recall was being at 270, (I have never owned a scale, but I would know I was getting bigger when my clothes wouldn't fit or when I went to the doctor). I was about 100 pounds overweight. Initially, instead of depriving myself, I decided to add fruits and vegetables as I knew I wasn't eating enough of them. That was my first step. I worked through stages that way. At first, I lost a little bit of weight — five pounds. I would get really excited and would add a new component to my program. I started doing aerobic videos at home because I couldn't afford to go to the gym. I ate fast food all of the time, so I made myself quit "super-sizing". I just didn't say, "That's it, I'm cutting out all the burgers and fries." I would just get a regular size fry and drink, instead of triple size everyday. By adding more fruits and vegetables, I found I wasn't hungry for other stuff all the time. I made myself eat five fruits and vegetables every day. I continued to lose more weight. I then decided I wasn't going to drink soda anymore. That made a difference, and I lost another 10 pounds. Then I would hit another plateau. I wouldn't lose weight for a while, so I would add something else. My weight has tapered down to the point where I now weigh about 180. I was 180 about three years ago, so I guess it only took me roughly three years. I moved from Greenville, South Carolina to Florida for a change, and that was probably one of the biggest challenges because I only knew one person. I was very lonely, anxious, and the one person I did know ate horribly. As a result, I gained back 30 pounds. I was very surprised because before that, I had managed to maintain my lifestyle changes. All of a sudden I said, "My pants are getting tight, I feel like I'm getting bigger again." So I weighed myself, regrouped, and just refocused on why I was overeating. I wasn't overeating as much as I was eating the wrong things — comfort foods. I would say, "Today was a crappy day and I don't know anybody. I'm going to go eat a donut." So now I've gotten back to the point where I'm 180.

I've maintained my weight for about a year now. It's not particularly hard. I was surprised when I moved here and gained some of the weight back, I got up to about 210. I wasn't anywhere near the original 270, but it was enough to say, "OK, I'm going the wrong way." I made the change slowly and incrementally. Those were the steps on how I did it physically. Mentally, I guess without being too detailed, you go through things, especially with the last 30 pounds. I caught myself looking in the mirror a lot. I didn't recognize myself. I would look in the mirror and think, "Who is that?" It is actually a little freaky for someone who has been pretty large most of their life to be smaller. You feel like you are disappearing. Like I said, for me it was never much about body image, as strange as that is. I was never worried about looking better, I was worried about being healthier. Mentally, there were some stages and some hard points too.

They seemed to correspond with the plateaus of weight. As I would work through them and tweak something out, I would lose another 10 pounds.

Concerning major milestones, I can't really think of one. Somewhere, I did make a dramatic change. For example, when I think about the way I ate when I started, and how I eat now, it is tremendously different. Somewhere along the way I made a complete switch. I don't eat red meat anymore. Sometimes you want something fried and that's OK, but not everyday and not a super size of French fries. I eat a lot of fruits and vegetables, which is so ironic because that is the way I was raised. I have kind of rebounded. When your parents tell you what not to do, that's the first thing you are going to do. So, I don't remember an incremental exact milestone moment when it happened. It was a bunch of little things. I would lose some weight and then I would plateau, and I would say, "OK, what am I going to do to fix it?" It was a very slow process. When I averaged it out, I probably lost about 1/2 pound a week, which is OK because I'll be able to keep the change.

My family was a great support structure, mainly from the attention you get when you lose weight. We all know how it is when you walk in, even if you haven't lost weight, and someone says, "Wow, you look like you've lost weight." That may be shallow to say, but it gets you going. It gives you that extra bit of, "OK — I'm doing it" attitude. People are noticing that I'm looking different. My family was very supportive. Actually, all of my brothers and sisters who were overweight have all lost a significant amount of weight in the last five years. We started this together, which is kind of cool. I think one of us looked at the other and said," We can do this." None of us are thin, but we are all within healthy weight ranges.

It was very important to make environmental changes in my home, car, work, and that sort of thing. At home, I learned to quit buying junk food from the grocery store. I knew what my weakness was, and if it was in the house I would eat it. I have a very hard time going over to a close friend's house where there will be donuts, chips, etc. and I know I will want to eat them. I no longer get dressed and go to the store to buy a bag of chips. As far as changes at work, I know this may sound strange, but I made a habit of not taking dollar bills with me to work for the vending machine. The vending machines are full of junk food. It seemed to make a significant difference. I pack healthy snacks.

I smoked periodically when I was younger, but I personally don't think it was tremendously habit forming. I would smoke when I was really nervous or anxious, and I was a social smoker. I never became horribly hooked. Smoking started to give me headaches, so I just quit. I don't know if I consider that a major health change because I was never completely hooked.

I feel like my mom was my role model, as far as watching her healthy way of eating and living. My older sister, though, impressed me most with her behavior change. When I was an adolescent, she was overweight, and she went through a lot. I think it just made me realize that it was doable even though she yo-yoed back and forth for a while before she finally lost the weight for good. It made a big difference to know that there was somebody that could successfully do it. My motivation for making the change was my health. I have memories of when I couldn't sit in an airplane seat or a roller coaster ride.

I didn't see myself as overweight when I looked in the mirror, but when somebody would take a picture of me, I would look at the picture and think, "Oh my God, I am huge." It really just dawned on me the day my mobility was affected; when I was having a hard time moving, getting up and down, or crossing my legs. That was pretty much it; it was really just a health factor.

By the time I started to lose weight, I had my associate's degree, in science, so I had the knowledge. I've taken nutrition, as well as anatomy and physiology classes, so I already had a lot of the basic health information. I really knew how to lose weight; it was just a matter of figuring out what to do.

I went to a counselor periodically throughout high school. It wasn't just about weight, but we did talk about that. My mom had me see a counselor mainly because she was a single parent. I think she realized that I couldn't talk to her about everything, and he offered an unbiased opinion. I think the counseling made a difference, because sometimes he could be very blunt and point out how large I was really getting. I had a doctor and I received physicals, but I wasn't under a specific program that a doctor put me on. I did not use any medication. I started taking a multivitamin, but I didn't take anything that was a diet drug.

I think I was very prepared for making this change. As far as the knowledge and the support I had, I felt prepared. If you don't feel prepared, it's not going to work. If it's something that is forced on you, or you're not ready, I don't think it's going to work either.

If I had to do it again, I would probably partner with someone, especially for exercising. I did exercise in the beginning and I was always fairly active. I walk a lot at Home Depot, and didn't join a gym until recently. They did a body analysis on me about six months ago, which indicated that my fat percentage was fine, but I needed to tone more. You can lose weight which is good, but if you don't continue to work out, you'll lose muscle too. I think that exercising would have been a bigger focus if I were to do it again. I put a lot of focus on my food intake.

I really don't think I'll have trouble maintaining this change in the future, especially because that one relapse, when I gained the weight back and just swung the pendulum again. I feel like weight loss is a pendulum; you are either on the gaining side or on the losing/maintaining side. It's really hard to get from gaining to maintaining and losing. It's not like you can just start tomorrow. It seems like you've got to slow down the process of gaining, and get to the maintaining and then cutting back. Your body just feels different. My metabolism seems better. I feel slow when I am gaining weight. Because of that relapse, I think it made me more prepared to pay attention to the little stuff, and aware that it can sneak up on you.

I had a really hard time picking one personality type. I narrowed it down to two. It's hard to pick between the "Reformer" and the "Challenger", but I'd have to say, I guess I am the "Reformer". I am self-confident and decisive, but I'm not very confrontational.

My advice for others who want to make this behavior change, or any behavior change is: For me, any problem that I have, I break down into small digestible pieces. Have a clear goal. Mine was, "I'm going to wear a certain pant size," or, "I'm going to get rid of my double chin." It doesn't have to be pounds. **The incremental steps make a huge difference. You don't need to say, "Starting tomorrow I'm not going to eat any donuts or French fries for the rest of my life." That is too hard. Another big thing is to change your attitude.** Eating junk food was my reward for anything that was bad. **Now I use good food as my reward. When I have a healthy lunch, I feel better, and my body feels better. Making that kind of change in attitude about food has made a tremendous difference. So many people in this world know they need to lose weight, or make changes, but they don't know how. Small steps, clear goals, and working on your attitude all make a big difference.**

Donald S.

32-Year-old Male

Kansas

Quit Smoking

Quit Chewing Tobacco

Weight Loss

I am 32 years-old, married and male. I am a college graduate, and I have a daughter. I grew up in Kansas, in a middle-class household, as one of four siblings. My present occupation is in a Maintenance-of-Way Department. I currently consider myself middle-class.

The behavior changes I have successfully made are quitting smoking for over three years now, and I have also lost over 20 pounds that I have kept off for over three years. I also chewed tobacco for ten years, and ten months ago I quit cold turkey. I tried three other times to make these behavior changes before I was finally successful. It was hard because I felt like something was missing; old habits die hard.

My motivation to quit was from fear of having mouth problems/diseases, and I wanted to increase the health of my heart. My wife provided support for me through my changes. Also, people would notice a change in my weight and my attitude. They would advise me to keep going. I did not use any written materials or the Internet to help me change my behaviors.

My physician knows about my behavior changes, and was helpful and supportive. My physician would tell me that I was taking the right steps to having a longer life. I also had a role model. I do not think I will have trouble maintaining these behavior changes in the future.

My recommendation for others would be to look at the outcome you want to achieve. Keep that in your mind, and it will help you make big improvements in your efforts.

I would describe my personality as the "Achiever" and the "Peacemaker". My personality type affected my success because I set out to achieve a goal, and I achieved it. I also wanted to quit chewing tobacco for my wife. She hated it. My biggest motivation was always my family; my wife and our little daughter.

I am not sure exactly how prepared I was to make my behavior changes. I guess the timing was the primary reason I decided to change when I did. This was because my doctor told me I had strep throat and that I couldn't smoke for several days. I just thought to myself, "If I stop for five days, then I can stop forever." My job also required me to be outside working. The physical activity from my work was causing me to lose weight. Then I thought, "I could probably keep this weight off if I started eating better." So, that is exactly what I did, I ate better.

If I had to do it over again, I wouldn't wait for something bad to happen to show me I needed to change my life. The one thing that I would say was crucial to my success was everyone pushing and applauding my efforts.

Lori B. (sic)

52-Year-Old Female

Chicago, IL/Evanston, IL

Quit Smoking

I am single, 52 years-old and female, born in Chicago and now living in Evanston, Illinois. I quit smoking after 20 years.

I quit smoking cold turkey. Because I know how I am, I knew that I needed to have a foolproof strategy to do this. Otherwise, I would fail. For my strategy, I used a friend as my role model. I wanted to be successful. I smoked for many years but never tried to quit. I knew that if I was going to try, I would have to be successful at it. The catalyst in my quitting was a good friend of mine who, at the time, had quit. It was about six months later and she was still refraining from smoking. I was very impressed with that and thought, if she could do it, so could I.

I had been cutting down the amount of cigarettes for the last six months before quitting. I would say that a year before quitting, I was smoking a cigarette or two a day, I was hanging on to this. Finally, I just chose a day and stopped smoking.

I wanted to quit for health reasons. I didn't want to be a 60 or 70-year-old person coughing and hacking and possibly dying of lung cancer. **There is a lot of information on how bad cigarettes are for your health, and smoking is now more noticed by people.** A more restrictive policy at work also helped my decision.

I am a vegetarian, and that provided me with another reason to quit. I would think to myself, "I am a vegetarian, why am I smoking?" So I just wanted to have a different image of myself and be healthier.

I had always wanted to join a yoga center and adopt that lifestyle, so I used that as my motivation for quitting. Also, I couldn't see myself doing yoga and then saying "Excuse me, I need to go have a cigarette." I really wrapped myself up in this yoga lifestyle. I think without that I would not have been successful. I didn't want to replace cigarettes with another bad habit like over-eating, so I focused my mind on something else. I wanted to strengthen my mind. So, that is what I did!

There is a lot of information on how bad cigarettes are for your health, and smoking is now more noticed by people.

My mother smoked cigarettes, but my siblings and I never saw her smoking. She would smoke when we were in school. The house never smelled of smoke. But she always had cigarettes in her purse. I know because I used to snitch them. A lot of people smoke in my family. You would see them getting together on weekends, at card parties, weddings or whatever, and that's when they would smoke. I think it was more of a social thing. I am sure I looked at them and thought, "Oh they are grown up, they are smoking. If I am smoking I will be grown up too." Another reason I started smoking was peer pressure when I was a teenager.

I first started thinking about quitting in the late 80's. I was working as a typesetter in the 70's and 80's when you could smoke freely in the workplace. The typesetting field is male dominated, and everyone smoked. I quit in 1991, and I can remember how horrible it was. I had such a hard time sitting there at work. I would go over in the corner and just stay there, but it was very difficult to be in a smoking environment all day long and not smoke. I had to make environmental changes at home, in my car and at work. I eventually left the typesetting job and started working part-time when I went back to school. I stopped hanging around bars because they were smoke-filled and I also stopped drinking alcohol. I would pair alcohol with cigarettes. I stopped drinking for years. I was not a big drinker, but when hanging out with friends we would go out for a beer. So, I had to make some other lifestyle changes to be successful at quitting smoking. **I lost a good girlfriend because she was a smoker. She didn't "get" what I was doing. We would sit across from each other in a restaurant and she'd smoke. The smoke would be right in my face. I finally had to end that friendship.**

I also ended my relationship with my boyfriend at the time because he was a smoker. What amazed me was the number of non-smoking friends I had who were never bothered by my smoking. After I quit we would talk about it and I would thank them for putting up with my smoking and being supportive when I was quitting. So, I did have some big changes in my life.

The yoga community also served as a support structure, but they didn't even know I had just quit smoking. I have heard that nicotine leaves your body in three days, and that is really true. Once you get past three days, you are not craving cigarettes for the nicotine addiction. You are craving it for everything else, including every other reason you used them in your daily life. Those are all the things that you have to look at and re-assign some kind of value to.

I never did relapse. Right after I stopped smoking, I bought herbal cigarettes from the health store. I was sitting there taking these little puffs of the herbal cigarettes and said to myself, "What are you doing? You don't need to do this." It was very hard at first, but you know, every month was a milestone. After your lifestyle changes, you accept your life without smoking and I am now thankful that I quit.

My sister quit about four years after I did. We were the only two in our family out of five kids that smoked. My mother eventually quit. She had smoked all of her life. My mother was funny; she said it was not a big deal for her to quit and I believed her. She said, "I don't know what people are going on about. I just stopped smoking one day and it was fine." She never did start again. Her main reason for quitting was because my father was diagnosed with cancer, and she wanted to give him more support.

Since stopping smoking, I have developed the "Research" personality. Had I had this personality at the time I was quitting, I think I would have read more about the subject. I did read how detrimental smoking is to your health, but I never picked up a book on how to stop smoking.

I don't think I will have any problems maintaining this change in the future. But, I still have a really hard time being around cigarette smoke. I can't be in a restaurant if there is cigarette smoke. Well, I can, but I don't like it. I still don't go to bars, but someday I might because I have heard in the suburbs the bars are really close to becoming "smoke free". They are even talking about "no smoking" in public. So I have been thinking, "Oh my gosh, maybe I will get to go to the bars again." Although at 52, I don't think I want to hang around any bars. I don't have that desire.

Concerning choosing my personality type, I highlighted the characteristics that I have and I was unable to choose just one. The closest was probably "the Achiever". I think that having self-control helped me a lot. I don't know what trait this would be, but when I start to think of doing something, I am pretty successful at accomplishing it.

My advice to others would be to plan for quitting and set a goal. First of all, **you have to really want to quit. You have to really, really want to. You can't just say "I think I would like to." You have to be able**

to commit to it to be successful. Also, it's not just the chemical addiction to nicotine. That leaves your body quickly. It's the other addiction…the psychological addiction; the addictions that you have built up for the many years you have been smoking — all the little habits. Also it is important not to be fearful. Start to understand yourself.

When I started smoking, it was for an image. I also partly quit for image, which is interesting. I am just realizing that now. When I started smoking, I am sure there were Surgeon General warnings, but the cigarette ads on the billboards, in magazines, and on T.V. at the time made smoking seem alright. People smoked in the movies a lot more and I saw a lot of the adult population smoking. This has changed today so I hope kids are less influenced. I know my nephews grew up thinking cigarette smoking was gross. They would never even think of doing it. They were taught that at school. I think it's wonderful that education on cigarette smoking is so much different than when I was a kid.

Donald T. (sic)

53-Year-Old Male
Charleston, SC/Doraville, GA
Changed Cholesterol
Increased Physical Activity

I am 53 years-old, married and male. I was born in Charleston, South Carolina. I have a Bachelor of Fine Arts degree from the University of South Carolina. I currently work for Home Depot as a producer and editor for their business television. I now live in Doraville, Georgia, which is about 15 miles north of Atlanta.

Basically, I changed my health behavior when I joined the Building Better Health program at Home Depot, where I took a random cholesterol screening. It was 217, on the borderline. One of the directors of the Building Better Health program asked me if I would participate in a cholesterol reduction program, and I said, "Sure." The basics of the program were to become a vegan (vegetarian) for one year and see, with a very strict diet and exercise, if I could lower my cholesterol. I think there were 30 or 40 of us in the program. We received CT (computerized tomography) scans, which are basically pictures of your heart to check for calcification. We also received a doctor's examination and counseling. I felt motivated to change as they did find some calcification in one of my coronary arteries, a very small amount, less than 10 percent. They told me it was not much of a problem, but to change my diet. I went along with this because the motivation was that if I didn't change my diet then, I probably would have a heart attack within 10 years at the rate I was going. My prior diet was pretty good. I didn't eat junk food or a lot of fat, but I did eat meat, cheese and things like that. So for a year we were on the vegan diet, and the outcomes were dramatic. My cholesterol went from

217 overall to about 155. My LDL went from 150 to 99. My HDL pretty much stayed the same at around 45 or so. My triglycerides went from 180 to 65. It was very dramatic.

My mother, who is 88 years old, has heart disease and my grandmother and uncle both died of angina. So, I have a history of heart disease in my family. About six months after I was in the program, my brother, who is six years older, had to go in for a triple bypass surgery. I realized that there is no reason I should "balk" at this at all. Some of the people in the program did not understand how they could possibly go without eating meat, cheese, or eggs. For me, it was not a problem. The hardest thing was finding different recipes for plant-based foods, such as soy and stuff like that. But, it was fun and I had a good time. My wife and I were both on the diet, and for the better part of a year, I was a complete vegan.

There are three types of vegetarians; lacto-vegetarians who consume some animal material like cheese and milk, octo-vegetarians who eat eggs, and vegans, who do not eat any animal products at all, which is what the program asked us to follow. It was not difficult for me, as I wanted to be healthy and bring my cholesterol down without having to take medication. It worked. My change was so dramatic and greater than the program cardiologist, Charlie T., ever thought it could be. As a matter of fact, he told me that my LDL was about 145/150 and that there was no way I could bring it down below 100. He said I could probably get it down to 130 but in my health situation I needed to get it below 100. I was able to do that through diet and exercise, which was very cool. I have pretty much stayed on the vegetarian diet. I have gone back to occasionally eating chicken and seafood. I had my cholesterol tested about a month ago and my overall cholesterol was 165, LDL was 99, my HDL was a little bit lower, in the lower 40's and my triglycerides were about 65 or 70.

I grew up on a farm in a little county in South Carolina, and I think one of the things that impacted me was that my parents basically didn't understand (of course nobody did in those days) a lot about coronary health. Basically, if there wasn't meat on the table, it wasn't a meal. For breakfast we had eggs, bacon and sausage, grits and butter. We had hamburgers for lunch and meatloaf for dinner, seven days a week, 365 days a year. But, we ate normal for the time, and exercised. Growing up on a farm there were always things to do — we weren't "couch potatoes". As I grew older I refused to eat junk or fast food as I began learning about nutrition, which my mother also had an interest in.

I made this change two years ago. I don't think I will have a problem maintaining this change in the future. This was pretty much a lifestyle change for me, and not difficult as I do not have an addictive personality. I mean if someone says, "Hey, this is really bad for you, you shouldn't do it," that is enough motivation for me. There are a lot of people that still continue to smoke cigarettes and eat fatty junk foods, and I guess they just can't help it.

My support system was my wife. For example, there is a lot of saturated fat in processed foods. So whenever you are buying food, you need to look at carbohydrate and sodium levels. My wife was very good about that. She started paying attention to what I needed and knew this behavior change was both positive and important to me. Also, Linda W. with the Building Better Health program at the Home Depot support center was very encouraging. All the people in the program were very encouraging also. Some of us had no problem making the behavior change and others did. My friends were also supportive.

I love to cook, so we don't eat at restaurants. I feel I am a better cook than most of the restaurants around so that wasn't really a problem. It is a challenge for a vegan to go to a restaurant, because you don't know what food you are getting. Salad dressings, sauces, and stuff like that are cooked with butter or margarine. They are hydrogenated . The only challenge I had was traveling; going to other cities or peoples houses where they were unaware of my diet.

I did not face any barriers or relapses. One of the things that we talked about in the beginning of the program was celebratory foods, which my wife and I still discuss. We went to the mountains this past week for vacation and had chicken one night, which we considered a celebration. So, one of the things is that you don't have to deprive yourself to eat healthy or lower your fat. You can be motivated and still change your life and reward yourself every once in a while with a piece of steak or chicken, maybe during a special time like Thanksgiving or Christmas.

I did not have role models. On my own, I realized that I had the very beginnings of heart disease and my diet needed to change. I felt I had to be my own role model.

I didn't attempt this behavior change before, as I wasn't aware I needed to. I had my cholesterol tested and it was always 210 or 215. It wasn't 350 or 400 as with some people. So my doctor said my cholesterol was OK, but not great. They have now realized, in the last four or five years, that it is just not the number of the cholesterol but the ratios that are important. You want to bring your ratio down. That's what they call, "Syndrome X"; when you have a moderate cholesterol level of 200, but die at age 58 from heart disease because your LDLs are so high.

I have also changed other behaviors such as exercising more. I had always been a fairly athletic person. I enjoy lifting weights, running and I love to work in the yard. We have over an acre of yard space so I do a lot of yard work.

The only thing I would do differently if given the chance is to have changed 15 years earlier. Honestly, if I had done this 15 years ago, then I probably wouldn't have the calcification I have now. They used to tell us to eat margarine because it's lower in saturated fat than butter. They didn't realize then, that hydrogenated oil is worse than saturated fat. If I would not have eaten margarine all these years, I probably would have been in better shape. So if I had to do it all over again, I would have done it earlier.

In terms of how prepared I felt to make this change, I felt empowered because I had the information I needed. I am also a very analytical person and enjoy reading and doing research. So I immediately began researching online. I also talked with people, doctors, nutritionists, and trainers on how to lose body fat and improve strength. Through the Building Better Health program at Home Depot, we were each assigned a trainer and a nutritionist to help us. The exercise component of the program wasn't as much of a problem for me because I was already working out. But we were given a strict regimen with the vegan diet and an exercise plan, which became very vigorous. It was fun and I lost 20 pounds in the first six weeks, which was great. I read everything I could find and talked to anyone that could provide information. I wanted to learn as much as I could. Knowledge is power, and it can empower you.

I am an "Achiever" in one sense. I believe in personal growth, but not in achievement in terms of climbing the corporate ladder at Home Depot. I don't care about that as much. I like making a lot of money, but don't care about being a vice president or something like that. Individualists are sensitive, withdrawn, expressive, dramatic, self-absorbent, and temperamental. I can be a very temperamental, driven and passionate individual. I wouldn't say that I could be put into any one of the personality profiles, but I think I can see parts of myself in about six of them.

The advice I have for others who want to make a change is to know that a behavioral change has to come from an event happening in your life. It has to be something like a divorce or death or something catastrophic like that. For me, the motivation was when my doctor said, "If you don't change your lifestyle, you are going to have a serious health circumstance within 10 years." Six months later my brother went in for a triple bypass and it was like, "WOW!"

My advice to people who want to change is that you have to find out what you need to do. Information is power. You have to want to change. I have always been a person who has prided myself on not being stogy or set in my ways. I think the moment you stop learning, is the moment that somebody needs to put you in the graveyard. You need to continue to learn and be open to change all the time. You have to want to do it. That's the bottom line. And, it can't be something like, "Well I want to do it on Sunday but I don't want to do it on Monday." Basically, if you are considering a lifestyle change, it's really not that difficult. It's not rocket science. With sugar, salt and fat out of your diet, you think, "Man, I feel better." Self-empowerment is also important. That's something that Home Depot has embraced, and it is the basis of our company. For example, we empower people to replace a light bulb, and next to install a fan, etc. We can help you do it, through empowerment. Home Depot is extraordinary. Their philosophy is that, as an employee, it is really important that you be healthy because they have made an investment in you and want you to stay working with them for a long time. It's just good business.

Lacey S. (sic)

38-Year-Old Female
St. Louis, MO
Quit Smoking
Weight Loss
Increased Physical Activity

My name is Lacey S. I am 38 years-old, married and female. I was born and live in St Louis, Missouri where I am a registered nurse.

As long as I can remember, both my parents and grandparents smoked. I'm the youngest of five children and all my brothers and sisters smoke. As a result, I've always been around a family that smoked. I never did like the smell of smoke, and always had problems with it. I guess, like a lot of teens, I tried smoking at about age 12 or 13 and continued for about six months to a year. I was an athlete, so I quit smoking until I was 18. I smoked again for a few years and then quit for three. I was at a party where there were about 30 people, and I was the only non-smoker. So, I started smoking again. I then continued to smoke for probably another seven years.

Three years ago, I just couldn't stand it anymore. I never liked people smoking when I was eating, I didn't smoke in my house or car. I think more than anything it was just something to do, stress relief, or whatever. But, I made a promise to myself that I would not be smoking when I turned 35. That being said, I went to the doctor six weeks prior to my 35th birthday and said, "I don't want to do this anymore." My father had died and my mother had quit smoking for a couple of years. I thought, well if she can do it, being a 3-4 pack-a-day smoker, I can too. I was only a 1/2 to a pack-a-day smoker. I went to my doctor, and like a lot of women, I was concerned about the weight gain. I worked very hard with my doctor and went on medication. For about two-three weeks, I was instructed to take medication twice a day, which was supposed to help me with my nicotine cravings. Because I was sure I wanted to quit, I only had to take the pill once a day, and was able to stop smoking 10 days after starting the medication. It worked for me. To this day, three years later, I have absolutely no desire to smoke. My mother still is not smoking, but my siblings and husband still are. My husband quit smoking six months before I did, and it was three years for him last August. But, he started smoking again in September.

Only one person smokes in my office. The one thing I miss about smoking is the "smoking breaks" at work — you get to be outside more. I was able to get away from my desk more often. Now I find that I'm stuck behind my desk more than I used to be. There's the social aspect to smoking that some people enjoy, and it makes them feel less persecuted when they're smoking with others.

As far as my family, I'm on my husband's and older daughter's cases as she smokes at the age of 21. **All the health issues that go along with smoking are nasty and the ashtrays stink.** I can hardly stand the smell of it. My sister is also a heavy smoker and I'm on her case a lot too. She's smoked for 30 years now and her dry, hacking coughing is bad. She has a two year-old grandson and I tell her if she doesn't quit, that I'm going to be the grandmother to her kids eventually. But the need for nicotine is so strong that even that is not enough to make her stop. She goes to the gym with me but cannot keep up physically. She has one excuse after the other for not quitting. Just this year she has picked three dates to quit smoking, but hasn't successfully kept them. I tell her that she's going to be dead before the age of 55 if she doesn't stop. After quitting smoking, I only gained one pound the first six months. I was really careful with every morsel that went in my mouth. From six months to the twelfth month,

I gained 50 pounds. I've since taken off about 38 of the 50 lbs. I exercise one hour a day, five days a week.

I can't believe how much better I feel since I quit. I'm not out of breath walking up stairs anymore, I can go walking with my kids, walk my dog; it's amazing the difference in how I feel. If we go to a local nightclub where there is a lot of smoking, I frequently have to leave. I can feel my lungs getting dry. It's kind of weird as I've been exposed to smokers my entire life. I feel the odds of me ever smoking again are between zero and nothing.

Before quitting, I had prepared myself because I was just sick of smoking. I was sick of people hassling me about it. I would think, "I am a nurse and telling people about bad habits in reference to their health, and here I am smoking?" I really kept sticking to the point that I wasn't going to keep smoking past the age of 35, and I followed through with that change. I think the hardest part of any behavior change is to make the decision and follow through with it. Everyone here at the office was really supportive of me, even through the cravings. I had support at home as well, which was really important. When someone would poke their head in and say, "You're doing great, I'm glad you're keeping it up," that really went a long way. It was more of a mental preparation making the decision to quit and sticking to it. **I was always thinking about various scenarios, what I would do if I really wanted a cigarette, and ways I could say no. I would scenario plan.**

While quitting, I would use rewards. For example, once I quit smoking for four weeks I would allow myself to go buy a new pair of shoes. That was a trade off, because I like to go shopping. For me, that worked. But more than rewards, I was really, really ready to quit. I was probably ready for six-eight months. I was never a morning smoker and that was a huge advantage. I could be up for four-five hours before I had a cigarette, which is unusual for most smokers, and why it may have been a little easier for me to quit. My doctor was supportive. He gave me medication and helped me hold myself accountable. I also had the advantage of my husband having quit six months prior, which made it a little easier.

We never smoked in our house, so that was never an issue, because I could never stand the smell in the house. It was kind of weird, being a smoker and you hate all the side-effects that come with the environment. I bought a new car within the time that I stopped smoking so I've never smoked in my car. Nobody smokes in my car. At work, you have to smoke outside so I don't have to deal with it there either.

Everybody I knew, other than the people that I work with, smoked. My family smokes, so even now I have three ashtrays at home because they all smoke. That was really hard. Luckily for me, they were very understanding. I'm a verbal person, so when we're out to dinner, I just tell them that they can't smoke. When we're in a car or enclosed place, I ask them to understand, be considerate and support me. The thought of even having a cigarette or smoking has crossed my mind maybe once or twice in the last two years.

For me, the first thing that had to go was the smoking. Once I mastered that, the other things like exercising and changing my eating habits were easy.

I had two role models. My mother quit and she had smoked for over 40 years with a three-four pack-a-day habit. She quit by using Zyban. My sister's husband, who was a three-four pack-a-day smoker, also quit. He quit "cold turkey". I thought, "I don't smoke as much as they do so I can do this." They were really supportive and good role models.

The only resources I used were my doctor and visualizing scenarios where I would really want a cigarette, and how or what I could do to combat these situations.

I think I was very prepared in this last attempt to make this change. I was emotionally and mentally ready to change, so I gave myself enough time to resolve any issues prior to my 35th birthday.

One thing I would do differently is I would have started eating healthier and exercising earlier. Also, I would have not assumed, after not gaining weight for the first six months of quitting, that I was in safe territory.

I do not think I will have trouble maintaining this change in the future. I have the personality traits of the "Enthusiast" and "Challenger".

In giving advice to others, I would say it can't be a decision you are not 100% committed to. For any change in your lifestyle you have to consider obstacles that prevent you from being successful, and ways to overcome those obstacles. You should write them down. You have to take one hour at a time. Find a support group, family, friends, whatever it may be. Use gum or straws; whatever will get you through. It's a lot easier to stop smoking and lose weight than to have a lung transplant. That's just the way it is.

Ronald W.D.

66-Year-Old Male

St. Louis, MO/De Soto, MO

Quit Smoking

I live in De Soto, Missouri. I was born February 16, 1937. I was born in St. Louis, and I have lived within the greater St. Louis area all of my life. When I was nine years old I moved to Jefferson County, and attended a two-room grade school. That was different than what I was used to in South St. Louis. I have lived in Jefferson County ever since. I'm married, 66 years-old, and have a college degree from Washington State University. I have completed some graduate coursework toward a master's degree. After a year of marriage, and with a child on the way, I left the profession of teaching to pursue a more lucrative career in sales. My sales career included selling lab chemicals, athletic supplies, and biomedical items. I have been retired for four years, and I am enjoying every minute of it.

My father was a disciplinarian, and my mother was a realist who tried to keep us on the "straight and narrow". She made sure we went to church and Sunday school. I had an older brother who started drinking when he was fourteen. My dad liked his beer too. From their behavior, I vowed never to be a person who takes things to excess.

One of the behavior changes that I am extremely proud of is quitting smoking. I started smoking when I was nine years old. At nine, I began picking up cigarette butts off the street and smoking them. That was during World War II when it was not uncommon to see sailors and soldiers smoking around town. That really influenced me as I wanted to be a "big shot" and a "big guy", like them. I also used to love going to the movies, which I feel was another influence. Everyone seemed to be smoking and I felt I had to try it too. I think I was about 12 when I first inhaled. I can still remember the experience. Exactly where it was, when it was, and who was around because it was such a horrible feeling. I began smoking more often when I was 13 or 14. My buddies were all doing it. Even though I was an athlete, I smoked throughout high school and college.

In my 30's I opened my own business. I started smoking really heavily, and was up to about two packs a day. This was thirty years ago, when the government began placing anti-smoking ads on television The ads didn't have an effect on me. Like other smokers, I had tried to quit three or four times and found that I could quit only for a week or two. I couldn't tell the reasons why I would go back to smoking. My kids were about five and eight, and would watch the anti-smoking ads on television. To this day, I can still recall them asking why I smoked. They could see that smoking was harmful. Their questioning gave me incentive to stop smoking. Knowing that I was both, influencing their behavior and not being completely honest with them when I would say, "Don't do as I do — do as I tell you," really effected me. One day, I had a half-emptied pack of cigarettes left on the dresser and decided not to touch them again — and that was it. I quit and never smoked again. It's funny how an addictive habit affects you. I've never read about addiction, but I'm sure anyone who's been addicted to a drug has pretty much the same experience. For years, I would reach into my pocket to get a cigarette. The smell of a cigarette was enticing — very enticing. But, I was committed not to smoke. For years and years I would dream about it. Now it's a real turn-off. For 15-20 years, the smoke still smelled good. One of the reasons it doesn't smell good now is because I'm allergic to it. I still occasionally have a dream about smoking. But, I think it's returning to the bad behavior, which is more of a nightmare than anything.

Smoking is the number one health behavior change in my life that I am quite proud of. You may be lucky and not have a smoking related health problem, but what is the risk? When you're a smoker, the risk is higher for emphysema and other health-related problems.

I'm also diabetic. I was 22 when I was discharged from the service and diagnosed with juvenile type I diabetes. That required change in my life. It really affected my ability to have the energy needed to do the things I enjoyed, such as playing softball and basketball. I would have to eat a candy bar before playing basketball to avoid an insulin reaction. Diabetes is a continual challenge that I now handle much better, partly because I've witnessed people who don't take care of their diabetes and their poor health status.

I've been a heavy eater most of my life. When I turned 30, my metabolism changed. I decided to eat less. As a result, I never gained a lot of weight and was never in a situation where my blood sugar was so high that it caused other health problems. I have some problems associated with long-term diabetes, but not many. I still have fantastically good circulation, even in my feet. I had laser surgery on one of my eyes 11 or 12 years ago, right about the time I had a bypass surgery. These major procedures indicated that I needed to be even more conscious of my health behavior before my whole body fell apart. So, I began working out at the YMCA three to four times a week.

I began competing in the Senior Olympics when I was 57 and have continually competed for the last 10 years. This year I took second in the high jump at the National Senior Olympics in Norfolk, Virginia. I started out with just the high jump, and then added the 50 meter dash, 100 meter dash, and even the 200 meter dash and long jump. My participation in the Senior Olympics has really helped me stay focused. At the event, I would see other people my age doing as well or better from the start. I would say to myself, "Hey, if I'm going to keep up with these old guys and girls, I'm going to have to do something about it." So, I began involving myself in more events and more meets. Last year, I was in nine different meets from Illinois to Utah, and took first place in the high jump in every one of them. Recently, I've discovered that I'm able to jump the same today, at age 66, as when I was 57.

To keep in condition, I joined Gold's Gym about three years ago. I work out two to three times a week — two to three hours per session. I do leg exercises to keep them in good condition. I mainly workout on the elliptical exercise machine, which is low impact and easy on your joints. I've always stayed in good shape, but not in good condition. There is a difference. I eat almost no fats; my body fat is approximately 11 percent. I quit eating butter, red meat, and salt. I believe those changes have allowed me to live longer, beyond that of my father or brother. My father died at age 55, and my older brother died when he was 56. Both had bad hearts. I want to continue to be active and to enjoy my grandkids.

I work with my sons. One has a farm, and we do a lot of work there. My other son has an older home that we are remodeling. Those are the things that I enjoy doing. If I go back to my old negative health behaviors, I will not be able to do these things. I know I have to take care of my body.

Many people are procrastinators, and I think that hurts them. I may be a procrastinator in some ways, but when it comes to working out I'll push myself. I find it challenging to get to the gym, but when I'm finished I feel a heck of a lot better than before I went. This is probably one of the best attributes of working out; the mental and physical way one feels after working out is so positive.

I think my encouragement came from my own feelings more than anything else. I know my wife was extremely happy when I quit smoking.

She has been very encouraging throughout. My mom was encouraged by it as well. My friends smoked, so they weren't encouraging, but I was encouraged by my own desire of wanting to succeed.

I used to stop at a local restaurant, drink a cup of coffee, and sit around "shooting the bull" with the guys. Everybody smoked there, except me. I found the longer I stayed there, the more annoyed I became by the smoke. After my heart surgery, I finally decided I wasn't returning. I know the second-hand smoke was not good for me.

My physician is very supportive and keeps tabs on my performance at the Senior Olympics. He's a real nice person, and I'm glad I found him. He's more up-to-date and interested in my health than past physicians and specialists I've had. I am using several medications to assist me. I take medication for my diabetes and blood pressure. I take generic medication for excitable people, and I take Lipitor to keep my cholesterol down.

Regarding smoking, I was determined that I was going to succeed. I was going to do just as good, if not better than, anybody else. But it took awhile to get to that point. As for smoking and what I would do differently if I had to do it again, I probably would have never smoked or I would have quit a lot earlier. For diabetes and exercise, I could have been more informed on what was going on within my own body. I don't think I will have trouble maintaining these behaviors in the future.

Concerning personality, I am the "Rational-Idealist" type.

Here is my advice for others: First thing is to find out what the consequences are if you don't make the health behavior change. Become informed, read, go online, and do research to become aware. I would also say, don't give up. Even if you backslide a bit, jump right back on the horse. Don't give up just because you have a setback, continue on.

Don M.

66-Year-Old Male
Increased Physical Activity
Diabetes Management

I am 66 years-old, divorced and male with two children. Growing up, I was one of two children. My family grew up in a low socioeconomic class, and I currently consider myself in that class. I attended some college and am now retired.

I successfully changed my physical activity and diabetes management. For me, a "successful" change is maintaining six years of eating well. I am a vegetarian, and since 1994, have maintained six years of exercising. I have also controlled my diabetes for one year, after being diagnosed.

This was my first attempt to make these behavior changes. My original motivation for making the changes was social. I wanted to meet people at the local YMCA, which I have.

No one provided support for my behavior changes. I relied mostly on myself, although I did receive some support from those who were around me.

I used written materials and the help of a psychologist. My physician knows about my behavior changes, but wasn't helpful or supportive. I don't have a role model. I don't think I will have trouble maintaining this change in the future. A lot of people at the YMCA are going through, or have gone through, the same thing as I have.

My recommendation to others is to plan on sticking with your change for at least six weeks. After six weeks, you will feel bad if you don't continue. **Your new behavior begins to feel like a habit after six weeks.**

The personality type that best fits me is the "Individualist" and the "Peacemaker". I am the only one in my house. I am divorced and my kids no longer live at home. There is no one that depends on me, or for me to depend on. I like to be around others. I am very easygoing, which allows me to be receptive to new things.

The source of my motivation was my mental health. After my divorce, I had to do something. When I started to exercise and change my eating habits, I felt like I was not very prepared. There were other forces, besides timing, that helped me make these changes. I was forced to adapt to a new life. I had to put my health, both mental and physical, at the top. I needed to change.

If I were to do anything differently, I would seek more structure and plan better. One thing that was crucial to my success was getting involved, and emercing myself in these healthy changes. I wanted to look better as well as feel better. I was not going to let diabetes get the best of me.

Susan L.

40-Year-Old Female

Omaha, NE

Diabetes Management

I am 40 years-old, married and female with three children. I was born in Omaha, Nebraska and have two siblings. I am a college graduate, now employed as a Registered Nurse, and we are a middle-class family.

I was diagnosed with what I thought to be a horrible disease. My father died from diabetes, and the disease scared me. **When I was first diagnosed, I was angry, then sad. But then I decided I was going to beat this disease, and do everything in my power to be healthy and live a long, wonderful life. I obtained as much information as I could, used support systems, and successfully changed my behavior.**

I have kept my diabetes under control for three years, without being hospitalized because of poor or mismanaged care. I made this health behavior change 14 years ago.

I felt like I experienced different stages while changing this behavior. First, I was angry; I felt, "Why me, what did I do wrong in my life to deserve this?" Second, depression; I was very sad that I was diagnosed. Third, acceptance; I finally accepted the disease and said I will take care of myself and not ever be hospitalized for poor management of my blood sugar.

My original motivation for making the change was — with being a nurse, I see many people live with the complications of this disease. Their quality of life sometimes is bad. My father died from this disease. This all kind of hit me at once and I realized that I did not want this to happen to me.

Doctors and nurses provided support for this change. I took a week-long class to learn about diabetes. There was one teacher who really helped me and my mother. I really relied on the support of the nurses and my mother most. I received a lot of personal support from my mother.

I used written materials to help me make this behavior change, but I did not use the Internet or the services of a professional counselor, trainer, etc. I couldn't say that I had a role model either. My physician was aware of my behavior change.

I don't think I will have trouble maintaining my behavior change to control my diabetes in the future. I made one previous attempt to change this behavior before I was successful.

I would describe my personality type as the "Reformer" and the "Helper." I am basically a perfectionist and want everything right. I'm very independent and head strong. If I were more isolated, or didn't care about things, it would have been harder to change.

My source for motivation was seeing all kinds of people with complications from this disease; such as blindness, kidney disease, amputations, and of course my father's death.

I am unsure how prepared I was to make this change. If I attempted another health behavior change, I would probably change my behavior sooner — and do it right the first time. The one thing that was crucial to the success in changing this behavior was seeking the services of an endocrinologist and general practitioner.

I define a "successful" change by seeing results such as keeping my blood glucose level in control, keeping my weight down, and avoiding any complications from this disease.

Richard S.

60-Year-Old Male

Texas

Increased Physical Activity

Diabetes Management

I am 60 years-old, married and male. I have three children. I grew up in a low to middle-class family in Texas, and I had one sibling. I now consider myself to be upper middle-class. I have a high school diploma. I am retired. My former job was as a control brand manager.

The behaviors I successfully changed were increasing my physical activity and controlling my diabetes. For me, a successful change means losing weight. I had always kept my diabetes under control, but could never lose the weight. For this behavior change, I lost 14 pounds in five weeks. Before this change, I had attempted more than five times to increase my physical activity level and lose weight. However, this time, I stayed focused and very determined.

My original motivation for making this change was that I worried about death. I am 60 years old and over 300 pounds. The person who provided the most support for this change was my wife. I relied most on my wife; she cooks for me and gives me lots of love and support.

I used written materials and other media to help me change this behavior. I read books and visited with a weight-loss specialist once a week. My physician knew about the behavior changes and was very supportive. My physician was actually the person who recommended the weight-loss specialist.

I did not have a role model. Some people from my church have also made this change and are keeping diabetes under control. Sometimes they exercise together.

To others, I would recommend not thinking of eating healthy as a diet. Get off the sofa and walk. Walking is good for you. I walk two miles almost every day. The most important tool is maintaining the goal after you've reached it and not going back.

My personality type is the "Achiever". I feel you have to be driven to accomplish anything and everything. **My main source of motivation is my grandchildren. I want to be around to see them grow up and go into the world.**

I was very prepared to make this change. The timing was right in my life. Being 60 years old is the right time for almost anything. If I don't change now, I might never have another chance to do it. **If I could do anything differently, I would be more accepting of help from others.** Nancy helped me realize this. Nancy is a fitness center employee, and she has been a true blessing. She has opened my eyes and given me the support I was missing. Another thing that was crucial to success was my attitude. I have a totally new outlook on exercise. Now my attitude is pure determination.

Jose V. (sic)

45-Year-Old Male

Antioch, CA

Changed Blood Pressure

My upbringing didn't have any effect on my behavior change later on in life. In our household we understood, from an early age, the importance of the quality of food in our lives. That's a positive impact, when you are taught healthy food is good for you at an early age.

My dad had high blood pressure early in life. I saw him take his medications everyday so I think when I was checked and diagnosed I thought, well, there are alternatives. I did not want to have to take medications everyday.

You have to work out and, basically you are what you eat. What you intake and your level of exercise is what determines the outcome when you have high blood pressure. I try to workout consistently and eat the things that don't cause problems. Those are the two variables I acted on, and they seem to be working. So far, I got off medicine and hopefully I'm headed that way. **(Caution — See statement at the end of this story)**

I have job-related stress. If it wasn't for Dow, where I work, I probably would have delayed going to the doctor. Coming into work, we had to go to the doctor for a routine employment check up.

During my check a nurse said, "You have high blood pressure." She sent me to the doctor, and that was the major event that made me decide to change my health behavior.

I knew that I was overweight and my eating habits were really bad. Additionally, I did not exercise. I knew all of these factors contributed to my problems, so when I was diagnosed I really wasn't that surprised or shocked. Although, no matter who you are, when somebody says you have this, it is alarming. You know that a lot of people have heart problems later on in life because they had, let's say, high blood pressure and you say, "I don't want to be that way." That's what drove me to behavior change.

We went to the doctor and he wouldn't let me get out until I took an aspirin. The next day I was running around. My initial blood pressure reading was 180/110. Now, it's 120 over 70 or 75, and that's with medication.

The first step to changing was hard. When I first started working out, you know it's not like an overnight thing. The first 4 to 6 weeks, I didn't feel anything. My muscles started aching because I hadn't worked out for a long time, so for a period my body was not adjusting to the regimen that I was going through. I didn't lose much weight the first 6 weeks, and it was a bit depressing. So, I started changing my eating habits. Then, after 6 weeks, I started to see 1 to 2 pounds a week drop in my weight. That kept on going for about 6-8 months, and I lost 30 pounds. That was the threshold that I leveled on and I'm still at that weight currently.

I started exercising on my own, no trainers, etc. I have to mention here that I have not been overweight all of my life. Probably 80% of my life I have been fit. Just the past 6 years I dropped the ball, and sat down in the office. I was eating all these fries and hamburgers, I just got overweight. In my case, I think it helped that I had a background in the early stage of my life where I was involved in exercise, and it just kind of came back.

Until age 30, I was very fit. After that, no workouts, and going to an office job where I was sitting down in a chair all day and just eating.

I work out at the gym, but don't have anything for the house. So I bought a treadmill. I would jog around the house, but then I figured I needed a treadmill for the weekends. I don't believe in those, "diet-for three days-a-week and then go and eat whatever you want" plans. You have to burn up the amount of energy you take in. I can't just continue with the high intake of calories on the weekends without getting some exercise also.

One major barrier is the inconvenience of the workout. It is an inconvenience for people our age because you work 8 hours a day, you go home and have the kids with their problems and homework, plus someone has to cook the food. It's an hour or hour and 1/2 to find the time to do it.

In my case, I guess I'm lucky that in my workplace there is a fitness center. What I do is work 8-9 hours a day, so I come early — 1/2 hour — and leave 1/2 hour late. I was lucky that my workplace allows this flexibility. Some people may not have the same situation. But if you can, work your hours so you can exercise during your lunch hour — in the same place where you work. Although, I stay longer at work, I found it to be convenient for me.

My physician made the point very clear. He didn't spend hours with me. He just put the facts in front of me without going through any major explanation, or going around the issue. He just made it really clear by telling me that if I didn't change my behavior, here are what the results will be.

During that first year I had to go back frequently, and he was very encouraging when he saw the changes in my behavior. He was very supportive and commended me on this achievement.

I felt very prepared to make this change. If I were to do anything differently, I would start earlier and never stop. People think, "Oh well, maybe we will start with the next meal or on this particular day." It's part of your whole life. It's a continuous process. You cannot stop. I don't think that I will have trouble maintaining this change in my life.

The "Achiever" personality type is more what I would describe myself as. Everyone's life circumstances are different, but I think one major goal when you're looking to change is to eat right.

The other thing is that you can't lose weight without working. So, the workout becomes, in today's life, the convenience. Many people don't exercise because it's a trick going to a gym. They have to understand that a workout could be anything. It could be in the house, or something simple outdoors. So, I don't know what would motivate some and not others. Each person's circumstances have to be evaluated separately. Then you see how you can manage your life or arrangement to include this change.

Caution: In an effort to allow each interviewee to tell his or her own story, all statements made were left unchanged. Proper nutrition, weight control, and physical activity are all part of an effective approach to managing high blood pressure. It is recommended that the prescribing physician be consulted before changing or discontinuing the use of any prescribed medication.

Renee D. (sic)

40-Year-Old Female

Omaha, NE

Overcoming Depression

Overcoming Anxiety

I am 40 years-old and female. I was born and raised in Omaha, Nebraska where I live today. I do not have children, but I have three siblings. I attended some college. Currently, I work as an administrative assistant. I have overcome depression and anxiety.

I live with my mother and serve as her caretaker. I believe my depression and anxiety began when I was a young child. My father was a brick mason who had a drinking problem. He would come home drunk late at night and start yelling, screaming and hitting my mother. They would throw things at each other — there were even dents on the walls from objects being thrown. As a child, I would hide the steak knives and breakable things. I'd go to bed in my clothes or with my shoes by my bed because my mother and I would run away from him in the middle of the night and he would chase us. My mother and I would try to find neighbors to help us. My brothers, who were quite a bit older than I, would also drive us to safety.

Ever since I was young, I felt that it was, "My mother and I against the world." I can still recall when my father first hit my mother. He hit her in the face on the left side where she now has a hearing problem. My dad wasn't mean to me, but indirectly I feel I was abused. My mother and father eventually separated. He did try to come back, but she wouldn't allow him. I was always scared of him. When my father wasn't drinking, he was a great guy.

Academically, I did really well in grade school and then average in high school. I didn't have problems with relationships in high school, although I didn't have many dates as I was scared of men. After I moved away from home, I went on a date and was attacked by the person.

At the age of 40, my brother started having marital problems. They would fight and I would see his children cry. I would have flashbacks of my childhood. This was when my depression hit hard. My brother went to pick up the kids for visitation and I would go along with him. He and his ex would fight and his kids would cry. I didn't see two little boys who were crying (his kids), instead I saw a little blonde girl (me). That really bothered me. I began to cry and sleep all the time, and then withdrew from people. My weight fluctuated. I didn't want to relive that period of my life again. I felt as though God was punishing me. My mother and brothers couldn't understand what was wrong. My mother copes by putting things out of her mind. I couldn't do that. It was hard to live day-to-day. Work was my outlet where I thrived.

The flashbacks went on for several years. My brother would call or come over and vent his problems, which was not good for me. Eventually, his ex-wife did not allow my brother or I to have visitation with his children, which was very hard on me. I went through a grieving process. I have not seen his children for 12 years.

Seven years ago, I began dating a man. I felt uncomfortable in the relationship, and as a result, began acting strange. We broke up three times because of my behavior. Things would set me off and I would throw tantrums, which he couldn't take any longer. It was then that I decided I had to do something about my behavior. I was either going to kill myself or never be able to have a relationship.

I tried different things to combat my depression. I used EAP (Employee

Assistance Program) services. I received six sessions free for one year. The counselor suggested I see a doctor for depression medication. I had anxiety problems and worried all the time. I went to a doctor and she asked if I ever thought of killing myself. I replied that I sometimes drive recklessly and hope that someone hits me. She was surprised at my response and asked that I see a counselor. She also gave me a prescription. I felt that she should have done something like put me in a hospital, instead of just having me promise I wouldn't do anything to myself. I felt that the physician was not helpful. I am still taking medication. I thought it would be a cure all, but I realized it doesn't cure everything. It does take the "edge off" and calms me down. I went to a few counselors but didn't feel like they were helping me. I went back to EAP, but that didn't really help as I felt they were just a sounding board. There are a few years that I can't really remember — it's like I was in a dark cave.

I have a great girlfriend whom I credit for most of my success. She would call every night and counsel me. Our conversations were different than with my counselors because they were more personal. She knew me and would talk as long as I needed. The other support mechanism was learning what triggered my depression. One trigger is hearing a man raise his voice. I have to recognize these triggers and remind myself to calm down. I have to stop and think of what I am anxious or depressed about, and calm myself down. It took a long time to learn this, but I now can do it.

I used material from the Adult Children of Alcoholics program. It helped to know that there were people like me out there. To cope, I do volunteer work and take dance lessons, which I have taken since I was five years old. I still take tap dancing. I love to dance and it makes me happy. At Christmas I volunteer with Operation Santa on my own time. I shop and buy for 27 people. I wrap and deliver the gifts. Last year, I went to a mentally challenged children's home. That affected me greatly and I cried for two days. The kids were thrilled! They wanted to hug me. It was awesome and a great feeling to see them so happy. I will do it again. My mother and I are both very giving.

I found that I collect things from my childhood that remind me of happy times. One thing that makes me happy is going through old photographs. I noticed there were a lot of pictures of me as a child, smiling with my father. I don't remember taking those, but I realize there were good times, and that my father loved me.

By the time I decided to reconnect with my father — he died. I was scared of him, so I was waiting for my brother to come to town and accompany me. I did talk to him and placed flowers on his grave site. I can now deal with the past. I would recommend that people find what makes them happy.

David E.

43-Year-Old Male
Western Pennsylvania
Increased Physical Activity

My name is David E. I am 43 years-old, married and a college graduate with two children. I am one of three siblings. I grew up in Western Pennsylvania. My current job is a Customer Service supervisor. I was raised middle class, and would now classify myself as upper-middle class.

The successful health behavior change I accomplished was increasing my physical activity. Previously, I never exercised at all. Now I work out at least five times a week. I made this change seven months ago. My original motivation for making this change was my health. I wasn't overweight, but I felt I could improve my health by eating better and exercising. There was this "Dump Your Plump" (see reference in Appendix C) contest, which was a 10 week program with 52 groups. In terms of support, my teammates supported me the most. We had to work together to compete and it really helped. My wife did everything with me as well. She was right by my side. I also used written materials and the Internet to help with this behavior change. Additionally, for the first three months, I utilized a personal trainer.

My physician did not know about this change. My role models were my team members. I don't know anyone personally who has made this change or who has given me the inspiration for it. I don't think I will have trouble maintaining this change in the future.

My recommendation for others is to set realistic goals and follow them through. If you can work with others, have a buddy; someone you can really depend on to push you when you think you cannot go on. My personality type is the "Achiever" because I am focused and determined to go from 25 percent body fat to 12 percent. Currently, I am at 15 percent. My main source of motivation was my health and appearance. I wanted to look better.

I was very prepared to make this change. I wanted to start at the end of last year, but I decided to wait for the contest to begin at the start of the new-year. It helped to have people around me aiming for the same prize.

If I were to do it again, I wouldn't do anything differently. It has worked out great. The one thing that was crucial to my success was perseverance.

Stanley S.

56-Year-Old Male
Lansing, MI
Increased Physical Activity
Diabetes Management

I am 56 years-old, married and male with one child. I spent most of my childhood in Lansing, Michigan. I grew up in a middle class home, and consider myself middle class currently. I am a manager.

The two health behavior changes I successfully accomplished are increasing my physical activity and gaining better control of my diabetes. I had tried so many times in the past to get more fit, so just the fact that I was able to do this and maintain it is a success for me. It took me two years to achieve successful control of my diabetes and to increase my physical activity. I had previously tried four times to change these behaviors. I don't feel like I went through any stages to get to my ultimate goal.

My original motivation for making these changes was that I wanted to build my upper-body strength. I was going fishing in Alaska and wanted to be strong enough to pull the fish out of the water.

My wife and my doctor were the two main people who supported my behavior change. In trying to reach my goals, I relied on my wife the most during the past two years. I also used written materials, such as the Internet and other media to help me make this change. In addition, I also utilized professional help. My physician was very supportive and helpful.

My role model is my wife because she is so strong. I don't think that I will have any trouble maintaining this behavior change in the future. **The recommendation that I give to people is — if you are diagnosed with**

diabetes, take steps to keep it under control. If you make positive changes as soon as you are diagnosed, then you could most likely prevent some negative things from happening. Good health is better health.

I think that my personality type is the "Achiever" and "Challenger". I set out to achieve. I like to take on goals which are a little hard, and accomplish them. I exercise six times a week for at least an hour.

My main source of motivation is the fact that I am very self-disciplined.

I was very prepared for this change. This change occurred because of other forces in my life. Age made me look at the future. I was not getting younger, so I had to change some things. Health is the most important thing. I had to eat better and exercise so I could control my diabetes.

I wouldn't do anything differently if I had to do the behavior changes again. One thing that was crucial to my success in changing my behaviors was that my wife stood by me through everything. She was there to push and support me. She is my other half.

Leslie P. (sic)

41-Year-Old Female

Kansas

Weight Loss

Overcoming Depression

My name is Leslie P. I am 41 years-old, divorced and female. I attended some college, and have no children. I have four siblings and was raised in a middle class family. I have lived all over the country, but mainly in Kansas.

I was married for nearly eight years. I had a normal childhood, except when my parents split up for awhile. I probably saw some things I shouldn't have. Through counseling, I became aware of these things. I saw my mother go through what I went through. I was raped. I ran away from it, which brought me to South Dakota. I became involved romantically with someone, but it was a bad relationship. I wasn't seeing things clearly. I don't know why it all happened. After I got married I knew it wasn't right, and after two years, it was doomed.

As far as my diet, we grew up eating healthy. My parents didn't believe in junk food. I didn't have problems with my diet until marriage. My husband was a "meat and potatoes" person. I was still very active before I got married, but the weight gain seemed to start immediately.
I eventually reached 190 pounds. I was overweight for seven years. During that time, the person I was married to continually put me down. There was no motivation to lose weight, so I never tried. I didn't feel good about myself. I was depressed and the depression became so bad that I would stay in the house except for work, which was my savior. None of my family lived nearby, so I was pretty much alone and did not have a lot of people

to talk to. I received support by frequently talking to my mother and family on the phone. It was a tough time. For me, "the straw that broke the camel's back" was when my husband wanted to seek outside relationships. Still not wanting to quit, I pleaded with him to go to counseling and apologize. He wouldn't do either, so I knew I had to make a decision.

I worked in a law firm at the time, and oddly I immediately went to the person I worked for and said, "I need to get out of this marriage, help me." My boss said he knew the kind of person I was, and that I probably wouldn't be happy unless I at least tried counseling. I didn't think I could afford counseling, and also thought that counseling wouldn't help. The next day, a woman came in to inform the lawyer that she was in a master's degree program and needed people she could counsel for no fee. The stars were in line for me. I contacted her and began to see her once a week for one year. She helped me a lot with my depression, and didn't focus on my weight. She worked on my self-esteem. I owe her for making me see that I didn't deserve these things. After awhile, I didn't need counseling and needed to focus on my marriage. I gave it one more year. I had changed jobs, and at this time, my father became ill and I went to visit him. He knew I was overweight and said that I needed to lose weight because heart disease ran in the family. I don't think it changed right then and there, but later I thought "If I'm going to die of heart disease, it isn't going to be because I didn't take care of myself." My father died a year later.

That same day I decided I was going to lose weight. I didn't diet, but changed my eating habits. I had stomach problems and went to many doctors. No one could figure anything out. **I don't have a scale, and never had one. I just decided to change the way I was going to eat. I had to lose weight for health reasons. I changed my attitude toward food and how I looked at food. It was the easiest weight I'd ever lost.** I truly listened to my body. The reason I was having stomach problems is that I was eating things I never ate as a child, so I started eliminating these foods. I don't eat red meat. I look at food as a fuel source, and I want to put the best possible food in my body. I didn't count calories, but started exercising again. Being able to "stick it out" was my attitude. After I lost the weight, I went shopping and found this pretty little black dress and thought "Oh, I'll never fit in that" but I tried it on and it fit perfectly. I finally went and weighed myself. I realized that I had lost nearly 60 pounds! I was, of course, happy. I felt really good, and my energy level went up.

My husband began putting me down for losing weight. He put me down for both, being heavy and losing weight. It didn't bother me, though, because I was taking care of myself. I never let anger rule me. I couldn't get mad, even with everything I had been through. The depression just kind of went away after that. The doctor wanted to put me on Prozac, but I didn't want to take it. My physician did know about my depression, but never talked about weight loss. He was trying to be helpful, but I wasn't accepting the help. I felt so bad about myself that I couldn't see "the light at the end of the tunnel". The only thing I could do was go to work.

My family was concerned about my isolation. Finally, one day, I woke up. I think it had to do with my father's death. I didn't want to put my mother, or anyone else, through watching me suffer. It was very hard to see my father suffer.

I don't think I'll have any trouble maintaining my health behavior change. I did put on some weight, but I think I needed to because I didn't feel comfortable at the lower weight. I'll never gain my old weight back again. A lot of it is my attitude.

My recommendation to others is to throw out the scale, change your attitude about food, and quit looking at food as a source of security or self-satisfaction; think of it as energy. Sure, you want something that tastes and smells good, but make it healthy. I cook great stuff with seasonings.

I didn't use the Internet or books. I used counseling for depression and my own judgment for weight loss.

Tim D. (sic)

49-Year-Old Male
Midwest
Increased Physical Activity
Weight Loss
Overcoming Depression
Managing Hypertension

I am 49 years-old married and male, with two children. I grew up as one of 13 siblings, in a lower class household. I attended some college. I am an I.T. professional who considers myself to now be middle class.

I would have to say my mom started me on the path toward changing my health behavior. She had asked several times if I would consider taking vitamins and diet supplements to see if I would feel better, and I agreed. A couple weeks after taking the product she gave me, I started to feel a lot better and have more energy. At that time, I decided to really try and get back in shape. I started by walking a little, and built up to several miles every day. Eventually I felt good enough to start running and exercising. I joined the health center here at work. I then started working out and running with several co-workers at least five days a week.

The behavior I successfully changed was increasing my exercise to at least three times a week for a minimum of three years. I also lost about 20 pounds, and kept it off for over three years. I am also over my depression, although it is still being controlled with medication which I began six months ago. I have also been off my blood pressure medication, and have not experienced any complications for over three years.

For me, a "successful" change is one that has a positive effect on your lifestyle, and brings happiness and tranquility to your life. Success is maintaining the change for life, which is the hardest part.

I changed these behaviors approximately two and a half years ago. I had previously attempted behavior change five or more times before I was successful. I felt like I went through several changes. I had several goals to accomplish, which included losing weight, exercising and improving my overall outlook on life.

There were several motivating factors that played a role in my decision to change. As I think back, general health issues played a big role. I had some health issues that may or may not have had a long-term effect on my future quality of life. So I decided to give it my best shot by not allowing these issues to affect my lifestyle; hence my "lifestyle change." Besides, I'm not a person that likes to take a lot of medications every day to maintain something that can be done by changing a habit or behavior. I'm also the type of person that, once I make up my mind to do something, I do it.

My wife and mother provided me the most support in making these changes. I think others supported my direction toward a healthier lifestyle, but I'm not sure that I would say they provided true support. In terms of whom I relied on the most, I'm not sure. I really thought that I was on my own many times. **Making a dramatic change in health, eating, and exercise is something I needed to place as a priority over the many other activities and habits in my life. Setting and maintaining new priorities doesn't always fall in line with others you share your life with.**

In general, I would have to say a lot of people noticed the changes I had made. Encouragement from co-workers, friends, and family members helped with some of the struggles. However, I feel that it was more of a personal accomplishment.

I did not use any written materials or other media forms to help with my behavior changes. I didn't seek any professional help either, but I did use online resources. My physician knew about my behavior changes and was supportive of any change that proved to be healthy. We have talked several times, but I now feel that he understands and knows that I have made these changes.

I didn't have a role model. Regarding whether or not I will have trouble maintaining this change in the future — yes and no. Some of the changes are very hard to maintain, and I struggle with that everyday. Getting others to support your effort is also hard. Setting aside time for you is something I also found hard to accomplish.

I would describe myself as the "Reformer". As a "Reformer", I would say that once I make up my mind to make changes, I do it. This is typically how I do things that are not part of my daily routine. I believe in being satisfied with your life decisions and directions. That is the key. I was not very prepared to make the changes however, my source of motivation was that I was tired of being overweight and out of shape. I now enjoy looking in the mirror and seeing that I have met my goals and made accomplishments.

Timing was the main reason for making this change at the point in my life that I did. There were several things going on in my life prior to deciding to make these changes. Some of those events had come to a close, and I was at a point where I decided that I wanted to do things differently. It's not that I believe life is too short (and I do) but we can make it better and longer by changing our perspective. That's what I did. And, it's OK if not everyone agrees.

In attempting these behavior changes again, I'm not sure what I would do differently. I'm not exactly sure what other changes I want to make right now. Once I decided to make the changes, I set several personal goals. So, right now I'm on the path for completing and monitoring the first set. **My goals are always adjustable due to events you have no control over.**

The one thing that was crucial to successfully changing these behaviors was taking time for myself, even if it limited the time devoted to other areas.

For anyone making a similar health behavior change of losing weight, beginning an exercise program, increasing their activity level, etc., I would recommend being prepared and having your mind made-up that this is really what you want to do. If needed, get the help and support you need to achieve your goal. Take time from your day to work on your new lifestyle, even if it means not doing other things or going somewhere. **I found changing to be challenging, hard, frustrating, and not easy to do.** Realize this is a slow process. It's not easy. **It takes commitment, and without being committed long-term, it is not going to work.** If you have an "off day", take it in stride — make it one day, not an entire week or month, then get back on track.

Harold W. (sic)

49-Year-Old Male
Omaha, NE
Diabetes Management
Weight Loss

My name is Harold W. I was born in Omaha, Nebraska on July 5, 1955. I've been married for 19 years, and have two children ages 16 and 18. I have a Bachelor of Fine Arts degree in Photography from Arizona State University.

My earliest memory was being brought up in an orthodox Jewish environment. My grandparents on my mother's side were very religious. I believe my parents were bringing me up in an orthodox environment to satisfy my mother's parents. I remember thinking how unfair it was that I had to keep strict, religious habits and attend an orthodox synagogue when my parents did not. That was confusing to me. One thing I enjoyed during that time was the meals and all the doting that my grandmother gave me as a child. It seemed like she was always cooking big meals for the family. Eating got to be one of the safest things we did, and also one of the easiest things to do. I suppose some of it was healthy eating. It was primarily kosher foods. It was Jewish fare, and some of it is healthy. It carried our ancestors through thousands of years, so it must have had something to do with it. Consequently, I always carried around extra weight. Through my school years, I was overweight. I was overweight as far back as I can remember. I've always had those mental images of being overweight. I don't recall my parents being overweight. My father was athletic; always going to the gym, playing volleyball, basketball, and racquetball. When I entered college, I did lose a little weight because I couldn't afford a lot of food. I also bicycled for transportation, so I remember slimming down a bit at that time. After graduating, my poor habits returned and my exercise diminished. It became apparent to me when I moved back to Omaha and started working for my father. I ate a lot of fast food on the road. Then I'd come home, watch television and do nothing. I then ballooned up to my highest weight. A couple of years after that, when I went to work for the university, I started changing my behavior. I was diagnosed with type II Diabetes and I can point to that as a turning point; a real wake up call for me.

As part of my job, I take pictures of the back of the eye. As a result I have seen how diabetes affects vision, and the other nasty things diabetes does to the body. I went to a dietician, changed my eating habits, started an exercise program at the gym, and began bicycling and running again.

I do feel like I went through phases while making the change. The first phase was panic. I knew I had to change my behavior, and that was my ultimate goal. I had to change the way I ate, and make a lifestyle change. Then, I looked for advice on how to do it. Through the dietician and exercise program I stayed with that for awhile. So that was probably the first phase: just learning to manage diet and exercise, and learning how to get to that point. The second stage began once I knew that I could continue my health behavior changes. I would break the rules now and then, but was able to go back to my healthy eating and exercise, and maintain what I accomplished. I guess I'm in the third stage, continuing on, building upon and challenging myself by doing other things. I get up in the morning and I run, even in the rain. I take bicycle trips through Colorado and do a lot of active things. **It's sometimes painful, but it's fun. You choose your pain. You can either let your body go and have physical pain, or you can have your physical pain by running or climbing mountains — healthy things — and I choose the latter.**

At my highest weight, I was 290 lbs., and now I'm at about 185. I lost roughly 100 lbs. I didn't try to do big jumps. I just wanted to be able to look in the mirror and like what I saw. I had fun watching my weight go down. I just made it a personal thing. I'd tell my wife about it. I'd say, "Hey, I lost another couple of pounds." I did it slowly. I knew it was going to be a process. I gave myself a year and set a goal. When I met one goal, I'd set another one. So, it took about one year.

Family and friends were all very supportive. My mother was really proud of me. She just thinks it's great. She is going to buy me another bike as a reward. I'm going to run the NYC marathon this fall. She is going with me, which will provide support. And, of course, my wife is supportive. **My two boys, who are couch potatoes (they sit in front of the computer all of the time) are now starting to run and think about their physical fitness. So, my health behavior changes are filtering down, which is really validating.**

I did not make big environmental changes. I just have much more fitness stuff around. I did change my clothing, if anything, it would be my clothing. We started eating healthy and my wife wanted to lose a little weight, so we both just changed our diet. My mother is a vegetarian, so we patterned after her diet. I don't accept everything she does, but we were able to formulate something that worked for us and the kids. We eat a lot of salads, fruits and vegetables. We haven't given up meat entirely, but it is not the focus of the meal. We've achieved a balanced diet. We decided it was important to have sit-down family dinners, and it's satisfying to see our children like what we cook. In turn, they try and make meals for themselves, which are not frozen pizzas or microwaveable type snacks.

Concerning barriers, I suppose it would have been easy to fall back into old patterns, but I was real motivated. My peers wanted me to stay in the old patterns, but overall, there weren't that many barriers. Once I decided to do this, I was real focused and everyone seemed supportive. I would get depressed and go on an eating binge, but I'd wake up the next day and say, "Well, you know what works — and today is another day." It wasn't prolonged. I attempted to lose weight lots of times, I'd try different diets but they wouldn't work. I guess I just wasn't motivated and interested. It wasn't until I was diagnosed with diabetes that I became interested and willing to do it. My blood pressure also went down. I had eczema and that's now gone. My sex life improved. It's really been my second childhood.

I had several role models, such as some people at the gym. My father certainly is a role model for maintaining. He's been athletic all of his life, and he's in his seventies and is still that way. I find positive characteristics in people and try and say, "Oh, that's a good thing he does," and see how it relates to me. My physician, Dr. Wheatley, was extremely supportive. He'd say nice things like, I should be the diabetes poster child for being able to do this. He took me off my diabetes medicine because I no longer needed it. That was another goal of mine. I did not want to be on any medications. I had all the tools in place to do it, so I was prepared.

If I had to change my health behavior again, I would probably document it. Keep a journal of all the successes and failures; they are lost in my memory. I can only remember being elated by getting on the scale and being validated after doing a body fat analysis along the way. There were other milestones that I met along the way, but I don't have record of it.

I'm real confident I will not have trouble maintaining my new lifestyle in the future. I watch the weight and am real conscious of it. It's not overbearing as it was at first. When you start, you can say that you *have* to do this, but you should balance it out. It's not all take, its give and take. I've adopted that concept, and I can't foresee me ballooning up again. I am the "Enthusiast" personality type.

My advice to others is to find a comfortable and acceptable alternative to the behavior that you're changing, and master that. Then you can go back to that safe place any time you need to. Once you master that change, you can stray, not letting it rule your life, but if you feel like you're slipping you can always fall back on that. It's kind of like religion, I suppose. It is just a safe spot where you know what worked to change your behavior, so you can always just go back to that.

Marry Ellen Z.

43-Year-Old Female
Philadelphia, PA
Weight Loss

I am 43 years-old, divorced and a high school graduate. I have three girls and grew up in Philadelphia, Pennsylvania in a middle class family.

It was 2002 when I made the big decision to lose weight. I decided to do it, and stick with it this time for the rest of my life. I was no longer going to go back and forth with dieting. I had tried to change this health behavior twice before. At one point I lost a lot of weight, but then regained it. I went through job changes and setbacks that caused a lot of stress — then I reached a weight-loss plateau. I wasn't losing additional weight, so I became discouraged. Then, I was laid off from work and gained double the weight. I was rehired with the same company, but in a different department. It was the perfect opportunity because the job was in the employee fitness center, so now I didn't have any excuses not to succeed.

I made exercise a part of my life. I took it slow, ate the right foods, and did it my way. Weight loss had always been a struggle. I wanted to exercise a lot more than what I was doing, but it was hard because I was carrying extra weight. Eventually, I lost 67 pounds. I am most proud of how I reconstructed my body. If people knew what I weigh, they wouldn't believe it because I now carry my weight well. My body has changed, but I would still like to lose 70 additional pounds.

My co-workers provided support. I had many co-workers, and other people in the fitness field who educated me. The confidence of my family helped, especially my daughters. I did not use any written or online materials. I did see a counselor when I was divorcing my husband. I was upset with my physician because he kept telling me to lose weight, but I felt that he didn't really know me, and therefore wasn't aware of what I was already doing to lose weight.

I don't think I will have a problem keeping the weight off in the future. I feel this is who I am now, and this is the way I'm going to be from now on. My motivation was when I would see women, as heavy as I was, who could barely walk. They were my age and looked so young. **There was one point when I climbed a flight of stairs, became out of breath and thought, "This is it, I can't go on like this anymore!" My health has always been good, but I knew if I kept the weight on I would eventually have health problems. I wanted to avoid health problems — for my children.**

My role model was Kathy Smith in her videotapes **(see reference in Appendix C)**. She was motivating, and I wanted a slim body like hers. I read magazine articles about people making health behavior changes, which also inspired me. My husband and I were married 23 years. Even through divorcing my husband, I stayed with my weight-loss program. It proved to me that even though something tragic happened, I was able to persevere. I now know if something stressful happens again, I can keep going.

I would recommend the same advice that is given to those addicted to drugs or alcohol, "Take it one day at a time." I started taking Yoga classes, and I feel that it has helped me through everything. I feel there is a mind/body/spirit connection. I was proud to return to my therapist and announce, "I don't think I need therapy anymore. I am taking Yoga and I feel really good about myself."

The timing was right for me to make my health behavior change. I was ready, and felt that I had to do something for my health, and for myself. This behavior change is for me and no one else.

Kenneth N. J.

54-Year-Old Male

Queens, NY/Omaha, NE

Quit Smoking

Weight Loss

Increased Physical Activity

My name is Kenneth N. J. I was born in Queens, New York and now live in Omaha, Nebraska. I am 54 years-old married and male. I have dual graduate degrees in Public Administration, Education and Vocational Education Administration Supervision.

I was a pretty heavy smoker. My mom and uncles were smokers. Back when I was growing up, it was socially acceptable. I thought; my mom, aunts, and uncles smoke so it must be OK. I was 18-years-old when I started smoking. I tried a cigarette and became addicted. I think in my case, parental influence led to my smoking behavior. My mom would say "I don't want you to smoke, but it's alright for me to smoke."

When I moved away from home and was on my own, smoking was the cool thing to do. My friends were smokers too. I continued to smoke for about 20 years. I began thinking about quitting when I started coughing too much. I would cough and couldn't stop. My clothes smelled of smoke. When my kids were little they would say, "Daddy, don't smoke anymore." I had no stamina and became winded easily — all the negatives you hear about smokers. I also just got tired of it. I tried to stop smoking several times before, but was unsuccessful. I don't think the will power was there. I had also wanted to stop smoking because I knew I was smoking too much.

When a group of guys I was working with were sitting around a bar drinking beer and smoking, the only non-smoker in the group proposed for us all to bet on who could stop smoking the longest. There were probably 18 or 19 of us sitting around the table and, to the best of my knowledge, I am the only one from that group who hasn't started smoking again. It is one of those things that still sticks with me. I never quit, I just don't smoke anymore. That is how I frame it in my mind. If you say you quit and you go back to smoking that's "failure". So I just say, "I didn't quit, I just don't smoke any longer."

I thought about quitting at least two or three times before the bet actually took place. I went to the American Heart Association's, *Quit Smoking Clinic* (see reference in Appendix C). During those attempts I would start smoking again at social activities that were conducive to smoking. I would go to a party, grab a beer, drink, and have a cigarette. I knew I had to break that habit and knew the steps from the American Heart's clinic but I guess I just didn't take it serious. The addiction was pretty strong. **It's interesting that my children were in a generation where they were saying "Don't smoke," versus my generation where it was acceptable.** I grew up with all the television and magazine ads that gave the message it was cool to smoke. Take a look at some of the people smoking now, there are still some slim "model type" people, but if you take a closer look, most of them are "beer belly" type people. The "smoke outs" are also a big deal. When I was a smoker, I thought it was my right to smoke. Now that I don't smoke, when I am near anyone who is smoking, it gags me. When I am at a restaurant with a smoking section, I sit as far away from it as I can.

My daughter has also stopped smoking. She started because she thought it was cool. My son started smoking, but I think he's cutting back. I told them not to start because it is hard to quit. I told them, **"You may not see the harmful effects from smoking now, but in 15 or 20 years you will."** Smoking is also getting so expensive. When I was in the military and a heavy smoker, you could get cigarettes real cheap.

I also remember the days when you would go into somebody's office and an ashtray was sitting there. Even in the shop where I worked, you could smoke. It wasn't until later on in my career that smoking became a frowned-upon activity. By then, I had already stopped smoking.

To substitute, some people chew gum, some eat a lot. I tried chewing gum. I tried chewing tobacco for a few months, but my gums bled. Then I substituted beer and began eating too much, which led to my weight gain and becoming lethargic. I gained about 40-50 pounds. I wasn't exercising or eating correctly, and doing all the wrong things. The hardest part was probably the first three-four weeks because the urge to smoke is so strong. I was pretty cranky. For example, at work, this fellow named Terry was coming from the other direction, down a narrow corridor, where I was walking. I am not very tall or big. I am maybe 5'6, 160 pounds, back then probably 140. Terry was probably 6'6 and 250 pounds, he was big. He also had a mean look about him when he wanted. So I am reading my paperwork, not paying attention and he's coming toward me. Suddenly, we are standing there, meeting half-way, as I look up, I am looking at his navel. I slowly looked up, cocked my head and said, "Terry, don't screw with me." He actually backed up and everybody started laughing. Like I said, the first several weeks, cravings were very, very, strong. I would be at my desk and have a cigarette lit at my fingers and occasionally take a drag, but most of the time it would sit between my fingers and burn. Back then, I could easily smoke four packs a day.

During the first three-four weeks of quitting, I drank water and chewed pencils. Even though I had quit smoking, I would have an unlit cigarette, and would just hold it. For years I remember sitting at my desk holding something. Another habit I had was keeping a pack of cigarettes in my shirt pocket. I'd be driving home from work, reach to get a cigarette, and say, "Hey, I don't smoke anymore, what did I do that for?" I do remember,

I'd have a cigarette and look at it and say, "I can smoke ya if I want, but I am not going to."

After a while, the cravings became less and less and less. Occasionally, I will still wake up in the middle of the night and say, "Give me a cigarette." Even though it's been how many years now? I think anybody that smoked as much as I did, for as long as I did, knows it's an addiction, a kind of a craving that you will never really loose. Now I'm just doing other stuff.

To kill the time I would read a magazine, go for a walk, or do something in the garage or yard. I also learned to just sit and really enjoy life. At first, being around my friends and co-workers who were also quitting was kind of strange because everybody was real cranky. Slowly, one-by-one, you could tell who started smoking again. They didn't try to break me or anything. We continued to hang out together, but they continued to smoke.

Regarding support from my family, my wife had also quit smoking. If she had still been a smoker, I would have probably continued to smoke. The fact that she wasn't smoking and knowing I wanted to stop helped. She stopped smoking before I did, and when she was pregnant she didn't smoke. We didn't smoke around the kids. I would go in the kitchen or dining room and, if the kids were there, I'd go on the back porch. My kids were little so they probably didn't really understand, but my wife was supportive. While quitting, I was on the flight line. You can't smoke around aircraft so the crew chiefs would chew tobacco. At that time, it was also part of an image, being cool, being one of the guys. From that point of view, maybe I am rationalizing, but I bonded with some of the people I was working with. But after a while, I also quit chewing tobacco. That got old too.

After a year, I patted myself on the back and said, "Hey, I've gone a year now, this is alright." To some of my co-workers, I would say, "I had my last cigarette a year ago, and they would say, "Hey good." It is now close to 20 years since I had a cigarette.

I started running and changed my diet. I also lost weight. One day, maybe four or five years after I had quit smoking, I had gained weight and decided to start exercising, so I began to run. **I ran down to the end of my block which was a very, very short block. I mean very short. I was so winded and thought, "Something's got to change here." I began walking until I built up endurance to jogging. I can now complete an eight-nine minute mile for six miles with no problem. Now running has become my addiction. (Caution — See statement at the end of this story)** At the same time, I picked up Prevention magazine (see reference in Appendix C). As part of my subscription, they sent me a little booklet called 101 Ways to Loose Weight (see reference in Appendix C), which I read twice. I began implementing dietary changes, such as decreasing fat from my diet. Before, I was eating all wrong; skipping breakfast, eating a big lunch, a big dinner, along with snacking and drinking beer all night. It doesn't take too long before you put on the weight eating that way. My motivation for addressing the weight issue was that I just felt like crap. I was lethargic, my clothes weren't fitting, and I felt like I didn't have energy. I was basically fed up with feeling tired all the time. My clothes wouldn't fit and what really did it was when I saw a photograph of myself and said, "Damn, that guy is fat." And, that guy was me; I had a double chin and everything.

I tried diet pills, starvation, and calorie input. I starved and just didn't feel too good. While on the diet pills, I did lose weight, but I didn't feel good taking the pills. My heart was racing and I felt anxious. I had all the possible side effects. I educated myself, and began to eat sensibly. It took me a long time to become out of shape and gain that weight, and it would take me that long or longer to get in shape and lose the weight. My neighbors saw me after I had lost a lot of weight, and they thought I had cancer because I had lost so much weight in a short period. The last 10 pounds were the hardest to lose.

If I had it to do over again, I wouldn't have started smoking and had healthier exercise and eating habits earlier. I still have some unhealthy eating habits, but not nearly as bad. My reward for completing a marathon is I get a big old greasy hamburger. That's my motivation. The best thing people can do is not start smoking; live fast and die young.

I do not feel I will have trouble maintaining the change in the future. The weight loss and exercise will continue. Running is what I like to do and if I can't do that, I will find a substitute.

To those who want to make a behavior change, learn as much about the subject as you can. Beware of the many weight loss gimmicks, especially with infomercials. Watch your calorie intake, ensuring you burn excess calories and definitely don't starve yourself. If I can do it, I am sure anyone can. Go on your own willpower and learn what it is that you need to do, and do it. Realize that knowing what to do and doing it are two totally different things. **If you really want to change, I think you can.** Is it going to be easy? No. Are you going to have to change your lifestyle? Probably. Are you going to have to do things a lot differently? Yes. For example, my wife went to a cooking class to learn how to get rid of the dietary fat in meals. With hamburger she was told to cook it, drain off the grease, and pour it in a colander, rinse it with hot water and that will help with the excess fat. We are still eating hamburger. We get that 96% lean stuff. If we go to someone's house for dinner, we have small portions of high fat food just to be polite. When we eat too much dietary fat, our stomachs hurt. Cut out fats and eat more vegetables. I would also suggest finding someone who can motivate you. Find a coach, mentor, someone that can help you, or join a group. In my marathon training group, we have those who want to run a marathon but have a hard time getting motivated to do it by themselves. The group supports them. There are organizations out there that will help you. Losing weight, I did myself. But, with running a marathon; if I didn't have the marathon group, or a

Believe in yourself, that you can do it. Don't tell yourself that you can't do it. Once you start feeling defeated, it is so easy to slide downhill.

plan, then I probably wouldn't have done it. I ran my first marathon in August of 2000, and since then I have done a total of seven. I am now training for number eight. It's my new passion, my new addiction. **(Caution — See statement at the end of this story)** To summarize, just **believe in yourself, that you can do it. Don't tell yourself that you can't do it. Once you start feeling defeated, it is so easy to slide downhill.** When I quit smoking, and it dawned on me that I had quit and the cigarettes were put away, it was like saying goodbye to a very dear and close friend who was always there when I needed them. You are losing a friend so you have to look at it that way and press on. Learn as much as you can about nutrition and exercise, and find a program that works for you.

Caution: In an effort to allow each interviewee to tell his or her own story, all statements made were left unchanged. The definition of "addiction" is to devote or surrender to something habitually or obsessively. An addiction is not a desirable state, even for a healthy behavior. While it is unlikely this interviewee meant to imply that running was an "addiction" literally, it is important to note this caution.

Joseph V.

46-Year-Old Male
Canton, OH/Noblesville, IN
Weight Loss
Increased Physical Activity

I was born in Canton, Ohio. I now live in Noblesville, Indiana. I am 46 years-old, married and male. I have a doctorate degree.

I grew up in a semi-rural environment and, by today's standard, I ate a lot of butter and eggs. Everybody did in that time. Growing up as a child in the 60's, there weren't known health consequences or risks associated with that sort of diet. I didn't gain any weight through my twenties. I think I had a high metabolism, but that certainly started to change when I reached my mid-thirties and started to put on some weight. I wanted to make some changes in lifestyle...especially diet and eventually exercise. I started with these changes the first time, at age 34. I know exactly when it was — my wife was expecting a child. I had been gaining weight and thought it was a good time to start exercising, so I did.

I feel that many times men gain weight, along with their wives, when their wives are pregnant. I had some extra time and knew my waistline was a little bigger than I wanted it to be, so I started working out. I joined a YMCA, worked out regularly and lost weight. In fact, there was a time when the weight was falling off so fast that I felt somewhat powerless to stop it. The pounds came off easy at the time. Then I backslid a bit and my waist began getting bigger again. I tried several times again, and now I am on, hopefully, a lifelong routine of exercise and diet. I would like to lose a few more pounds, but I am well within my target weight range as far as what the weight charts show. However, I would still like to lose a few more pounds if I could.

My most recent, and hopefully my lifelong change in diet and exercise, came when I had a two-year physical at work. Our company provides physicals every two years that are basically screening physicals. At that time, I weighed 224 pounds and I knew I had to get that under control. Also, prior to that, my blood pressure had increased. These two things combined, put me on an exercise and diet routine that I am sticking to now. I went down to 180 pounds, so I lost 40 pounds and have kept it off. I am a little over 180 now, but only by a few pounds. I haven't slacked off my exercising or diet routine, and I have maintained my muscle mass.

I have a fairly stressful job and was having a hard time sleeping. I could actually hear my heart pounding. I went to the doctor's office because I was concerned. The doctor said, "I really can't let you leave this office because your blood pressure is so high." **I was put on blood pressure medication and my blood pressure did come down. I stayed on the medication for a number of months and then went back to the doctor and asked, "Do people ever get off blood pressure medicine?" He said, "Well, it happens, but your high blood pressure is probably just a result of older age and you are probably going to have to just live with it." He was not answering my question. What I was really asking was, "What if I try to get off of it?" He reduced the dosage to half and my blood pressure maintained at a comfortable level. We cut it again, down to a quarter of what it originally was, and my blood pressure was acceptable. Finally, he took me off of the medication completely.**

I attribute going off blood pressure medication to having better control of my stress. I really tried to manage stress better during that time. I started exercising and those two factors, I think, kept me off medication. I have been off of it ever since. It was a scare, because the doctor literally told me "I can't let you out of here without doing something because your blood pressure is that high." I am off medication and have been for several years. High blood pressure and being overweight really drove me to change my lifestyle.

I am now very conscious of the fat and calorie content of everything I eat, but I am not a fanatic about it. I have several books on general calorie and fat content in common foods. I now have a lot of that memorized. There are many things that I don't eat anymore. I became involved in what our company calls the "Regulatory Function". I am involved with understanding governmental regulations, namely registering for crop protection molecules, and part of that involves toxicology and environmental chemistry. I learned more about toxicology and how bodies react to foods and chemicals. I became more and more conscious of how I should be eating and living. That helped change my lifestyle.

I think my blood pressure was attributed to job stress and not knowing how to handle it. There are many people that I work with who are on blood pressure medication, so I feel fortunate in being able to get off of it. As far as my employer goes, their strong commitment to fitness, health and living right has been very beneficial to me. We have a fitness center that I use. We also have a nutritionist who we can ask questions.

The sleeplessness was killing me so I decided that I had to do something to get control of it. One thing I did was stress reduction, another was beginning an exercise program, and the third was a diet control program. I did take sleep medication for a while to help me. When I went to the fitness center at work, the nurse said, "Your weight is 224 pounds," on May 7, 2001, and I said, "That is not acceptable." That was the biggest light that went on. I can identify it to the day, May 7, 2001. I weighed 224 pounds and roughly 25 months later I weighed 180 pounds. It is now well over three years.

My wife certainly has been supportive and knows that I am conscious of fat content. She cooks so that I am not taking in too much fat. It's always a challenge because I have two kids and that works in the opposite direction. Kids like high fat and high calorie foods, so it's a little bit of a struggle. But, my wife has been supportive, and helpful.

The same principles hold true when we go out to eat. I am very conscious of fat and caloric intake. I eat a lot of salads and grilled foods. I eliminated fried foods; I do not eat hamburgers, French fries or hot dogs. I never eat fatty salad dressings.

I think mostly the support has been from the company for the reasons I previously mentioned. My doctor encouraged me to begin an exercise program. In fact, he was very interested in my exercise program because he does something similar — so we hit it off discussing routines and level of exertion. He has been supportive.

I would suggest the greatest, all-around influence has been the positive support of my work environment. It would be a stretch to say I would be doing the same thing if I had to go to the YMCA or the local gym, after or before work. Working here, I can exercise on my lunch hour. It is very convenient and cost-effective, with a very professional staff and just a very nice environment, so I am very fortunate to have that.

Concerning barriers, I have commended the work environment however, lunches are fast-paced and often brought in. We have an onsite catering company at work that provides us with our food so you often have to eat what is given to you. Also there are always snacks at meetings, cookies, and sweet roles, and they are tempting. I wouldn't say they are barriers. They are temptations that I have just had to have the willpower to overcome. I haven't had any barriers that I have not been able to overcome. If there had been, I would not be here giving you this success story. While I am happy to have made healthy changes, I don't really consider my situation that noteworthy or spectacular.

Patty R.

49-Year-Old Female
Pittsburg, CA/Antioch, CA
Weight Loss

I was born in Pittsburgh, California and now live in Antioch, California. I am 49 years-old, female, married, and have a high school education.

My mother only weighed 80 lbs. So, my weight gain had nothing to do with heredity. We weren't big eaters. My mother and father were married 25 years. Not too dysfunctional, just a normal-dysfunctional family; nothing that I'd go back and say, "That's why I ate like I did."

I grew up in the 1960's. Dinner was at 5:00 p.m. every night and the thing I remember most was there was always a stack of bread with dinner. We had a slice of bread and butter with every meal. We ate breakfast, lunch and dinner together. That's just the way a family ate at that time. I don't think my eating pattern came from my upbringing. I would gain weight when my mother couldn't.

When I moved out and got married, I was going to eat whatever I wanted whenever I wanted. I was going to let my water run when I washed dishes, and do everything opposite of the rules I had growing up at home. I did the total opposite of what my mother did. Every light in the house was on. If we sneezed, my mother took us to the doctors. She raised us the right way, but I totally went against her values.

When I had kids, I had to lose 50 pounds, so I went on a diet. I was basically a yo-yo — when I had to lose weight it came off, but I would then gain it back. When I was almost 40, the weight wasn't coming off. I think I was about 37 and had remarried. We were going through in-vitro, and with all the hormone drugs, my weight started going up and wasn't coming off like when I was younger. My weight kept getting higher and higher. My husband didn't care, so I didn't care, and I got up to about 240 lbs.

My doctor informed me that I had to have surgery on my legs because of my excess weight. I was working on cement floors, my back hurt, and I'd have back spasms. So, I couldn't work on terminals like I use to. I also had high blood pressure and migraine headaches. I was going once a month to get Demerol injections for my back, and then I was prescribed another drug for my headaches. One day I was over at my daughter's girlfriend's house and she called my name. I turned around, and she took my picture. About a week later when she brought me the picture, I looked at it and said "Oh, my God!" The next morning I actually looked into having my stomach stapled, because of course, I wanted the easy way out, but it was like $20,000. I wanted to wake up and be thin because I thought there's no way I could do it myself. I thought losing 100 pounds would take forever. The next morning, I went to Jenny Craig (see reference in Appendix C) and I was ready — this was it. I joined, didn't cheat and the weight came off pretty fast. When I lost about 50 pounds I changed my style of clothes, and it was almost like I woke up and transformed myself. People weren't quite sure what was different until I wore new clothes. I went from a Size 22 to a 12, where I'm at right now.

That picture was my wake-up call. I lost a total of 49 inches. I no longer get headaches. I didn't realize how health related problems were linked to being overweight until I actually lost weight. Before I lost weight, I couldn't sleep, but now I sleep fine. The energy I now have is great. Before, I couldn't walk. I knew I had to walk on this program, but I couldn't even walk. Now I walk six miles with no problem — there's no stopping me now. I have slowed down because the majority of the weight is off and I'm happy with the way I look. I wasn't in a life-threatening position where I was forced to go on a diet, but I didn't realize how much my health was affected.

I call Jenny Craig a lazy person's diet because you don't have to think, you don't have to count, you don't have to weigh. It's all about their prepared foods. There's a menu and you buy your food from there. I'm afraid to go off of it. I still have 15 pounds to go, but I'm afraid. This is the best diet for me. It might not be the best option for other people, but it works for me because I didn't have to think. The menu tells me exactly what to eat for breakfast, lunch, dinner, and in between. When I was thirsty, I used to drink Pepsi and I thought, "There's no way I'm going to give up my Pepsi." But once I had to start drinking water, I rarely had Pepsi. I can count on one hand over this last year when I had a Pepsi, and I originally had no intention of giving that up.

My husband, who is also overweight, use to look at my food and say, "I wish I could eat that garbage" or "To bad I can't eat that," and then I'd say, "Well, when you're ready, you'll be able to." Then I'd let it go. One night he said, "I couldn't sleep last night," and I said, "When you lose weight, you'll be able to sleep." And then he said, "Well, it wasn't that...I was hot." I said, "Well, when you lose weight, you won't be so hot." Finally, six months later he started losing weight after he saw the change I made. He's lost 48 pounds, and a total of 29 inches. He did it because he kept seeing the positive results in me. He kept making excuses not to do it. You just can't make a change until you're absolutely ready. For example, every Monday I would want to go on a diet and every Tuesday it was donut day at work. So it would last until Tuesday. My husband started seeing a big change in me after six months. Then he started the program and now he's committed to it, just as much as I am.

Jenny Craig did not push exercise because I wanted to look at pounds — I wanted to look at numbers first, and didn't want to be overweight and be going to a gym. I was focused on dropping pounds, and once you start exercising your weight loss slows down because you gain muscle and I wasn't ready for that. **(Caution — See statement at the end of this story)**

After a while I started at Curves (see reference in Appendix C). I now go to Curves five days a week. My husband goes to the gym at work. At first, we just started with the walking because we were not ready to build muscle. The other thing being overweight affects is going out more. I didn't go many places because I was embarrassed by the way I looked. But now, I'm out all the time, and that makes a big difference. My husband is now starting to come out more and more too. It's been a major life change. My daughter who is 29 years old just moved out in November for the first time in her life, and that's a big change too. I'm going to be 50 in October, and let me tell you, I'm not having an easy time accepting that. So, I want to look my best when I turn 50.

I now look totally different. Someone said I don't like those funny commercials with before and after pictures because you see those pictures of a person, and then you see them now and they don't even look the same.

I now look totally different. One time when I was at Curves, someone said I don't like those funny commercials with before and after pictures because you see those pictures of a person, and then you see them now and they don't even look the same. So I whipped out my pictures and they said, "Oh, my God!" I said, "It is true. You completely look different." I didn't keep my hair short before because it made me look fatter. Now, my look is completely different. In fact, some people no longer even recognize me. One lady I ran into was ignoring me. I didn't think that she didn't recognize me, but she finally realized it was me. I have a big family function coming up and there will be a lot of relatives I haven't seen since I lost the weight. So for me, that's my "coming out" party, and I'm really anxious about it.

Now, with losing the weight, I'm back into blues (industrial work attire).

Before, I wouldn't put blues on at work. I'm not required to wear them, but I feel with wearing them, I can get really physical and do the work in the warehouse. **My weight loss has made me perform much better at work. I was also getting hurt before. If you look at my employment accident record, I was getting hurt quite a bit. I pulled my back or hurt my back because I was working out in terminals with the hose, and I contributed a lot of problems in doing my job with the excess weight.**

When I started losing weight, it wasn't like I said, "I have to lose 100 pounds." My first goal was to be less than 200 pounds, so they weren't really big goals that could discourage me. It was like, "I can't wait until I'm less than 200 pounds." Now I hear bits and pieces of how people viewed me, and some described me as "a barrel". I wasn't supposed to hear that, but I did. The first goal also had to do with my nephew who is graduating from high school. I told my sister I'd do whatever she wanted. My goal was to lose this weight to go on their Disneyland trip. That was my main goal when I started Jenny Craig. I was going to Disneyland. Like the football players say: "I'm going to Disneyland" after they win the Super Bowl. I was going to Disneyland. That was my big overall reward. My next goal was to lose 50 pounds by the time my God-child got married, and I had lost 60. Now I weigh 152, and my next goal is just to get out of the 150's. I feel like I'm so close.

My family was so supportive. The people I work with, the women in the office, have been as well. It's been unbelievable. Without that, I don't think I could have done it. The compliments still come in everyday.

If you open my freezer, it's just Jenny Craig. My granddaughter is seven, and she came over and said, "Nana, you don't have any food in the house." So I went and bought her some snacks, and I don't have any problem with those. But otherwise, we go to the store every other day and buy apples, bananas, other fruits and broccoli. That's really amazing for us because we never really had that kind of food. There's hardly any junk food in the house. When I'm hungry, I snack on green beans and I mean, that is not me!

In terms of barriers, my first holiday was Thanksgiving. The guests were saying, "Look at this cheesecake" and I had absolutely no problem. However, this one time, a guy I share an office with brought in steak and warmed it up, I thought I was going to die. If I was going to cheat, it was going to be with a nice steak, not chocolate or cake or something like that. I would have loved a steak but I got past it real quick. At $100/week (for Jenny Craig) I didn't have any relapses or give in to temptations. When I was ready, I was ready. There was no changing me. It wasn't like I would diet and fail, diet and fail. I didn't do that. When I decided it was time, it was time. I figure I will spend thousands of dollars by the time I complete this program; but the weight is going to stay off. I'm not going to cheat and then go back to Jenny Craig. It would be embarrassing, depressing and expensive. This was my first attempt to lose weight. I wanted to lose weight before, and I debated it in my head, but I didn't try.

I haven't had fast foods since March of last year. It was so easy for my husband and I to get a hamburger on the way home from work. They built an *In and Out Burger* (which has delicious burgers) over here and I still haven't had one. I have not had any fast food. Financially, even if you figure that we're both on it for $100/week each, we've saved so much money because we don't drink sodas, and don't eat fast food. Fast food is very expensive. It really adds up.

I did not have a role model. When I went to my doctor, she thought I said I lost 13 pounds. I said, "No, 50 pounds." And she said, "Did you do that on purpose?" it was as if she was saying, "Why are you doing this?" She never said "Oh, that's great!" I haven't been back to the doctor since I lost this much, she just didn't seem impressed. My husband wouldn't go to the doctor. He avoided going because he didn't want to discuss his weight.

My doctor never told me once, "You need to lose a few pounds." I didn't use any medications or any over-the-counter products. Once I made this decision, I definitely felt prepared for making it.

I would not do anything differently if I had to do it all again. As for maintaining this change in the future, I'm scared. Maybe that's why I've slowed down so much — because I'm afraid. I have to keep it up, but I'm afraid. I don't know what I'm afraid of yet, and I don't know if that's why I've slowed down. If I cheat (what I call cheating) it's overindulging in fruit or something like that. I have not eaten junk food of any kind or even a steak, just the Jenny Craig food. My weight loss has slowed down, but I don't know why; I don't know what it is. I'm so close now, but I'm afraid.

I want the fear to provide some motivation. I made this goal for myself over a year ago. I feel like I look fine. I'm in a size 12, which is a normal size, and everybody says, "Oh, my God, you don't need to lose any more weight." And it's like, "Yes I do," ya know? So then I'm trying to accept the way I look and just say, "Hey this is it." But then I set that goal. I've got to reach that goal.

The guy I share an office with asked, "Does losing weight make you a bitch?" My husband asks the same question because I'm more aggressive. I didn't realize it. It's not that I argue with everything they say but I'm just speaking up more. I would assume that I'm more positive in what I'm doing and they take it as "Whoa, where did she come from?" I've been passive for so long. The "Helper" personality type is the one that best describes me.

I knew all the pros and cons of losing weight, but I didn't realize how much it would affect my health until I actually did it. But the thing is, you can only do it when you're absolutely ready. You're not going to do it before. Companies should quit making this "no smoking" policy — thinking they're going to force everybody to stop smoking and become healthier. I think it's wrong. You can't force somebody to quit until they're absolutely ready. You have to get to a point where you're ready or it's not going to work. I wanted to lose weight for myself — not for my husband or for other people. It's got to be for me. I've seen other people lose weight, but it didn't inspire me to say, "I wish I could do it." It was a wake-up call. I found a picture and I never spent money on nice clothes. I didn't go to a nice fat store. I would go to Wal-Mart because I wasn't accepting my weight, even though I was heavy for so long. I'll never wear a denim shirt again as long as I live — that's what I would wear from Wal-Mart. I didn't go to nice places because I didn't purchase nice clothes. That would mean I was accepting being fat.

The girl who took the picture that inspired me actually felt bad and apologized. I didn't see her until after I'd lost 50 lbs, and I told her it was her picture that motivated me. Whether I would have woke up the next day and lost weight, or later on, I don't know for sure. My motivation and decision was all in that picture and I thanked her. I told her, "Thank you! You changed my life — literally!"

Caution: In an effort to allow each interviewee to tell his or her own story, all statements made were left unchanged. There are many misconceptions concerning how exercise impacts metabolism and weight loss. Physical activity is usually considered an important part of a weight loss regimen. In addition, strength conditioning is considered an important part of maintaining skeletal integrity, muscle tone, and general functionality.

Kevin M.

47-Year-Old Male

Atlanta, GA

Changed Cholesterol

As a pilot, I must have a yearly physical to keep my license current. After my father died (who was also a pilot) I started going to the doctor. It was a few years after my dad had died when they started looking at my cholesterol. Shortly before he died, he had passed his flight physical, but I don't think they checked his cholesterol. I started getting mine checked once a year by my doctor, until I started working at Home Depot and got involved in a program called *Building Better Health*. Then I got it checked quarterly. It was always high, but not bad until April 2001 when my cholesterol shot up to 249, with no changes in diet or exercise. The reason for the increased frequency of testing was that I got into the health program at Home Depot, and a study they were doing at the time. It was a year-long program, using a physician, exercise specialist, and dietician.

I didn't want to be on medication. I wanted to see what I could do with diet and exercise. I've always worked out, been athletic, and said I would stay physically fit. I enjoy outdoor activities and worked in commercial television, so I knew I needed to meet the demands of carrying equipment up mountains, or wherever we would go. Growing up, diet was always important. I consistently ate three meals a day, and we always ate dinner together. My mom stayed at home, we were from New England, and our extended family enjoyed food, and always had a big dinner together.

There wasn't a family history of heart disease until my dad died. We didn't have an autopsy done, but we should have checked to see if he had high cholesterol. I am convinced that high cholesterol contributed to his death. My brother has high cholesterol, and is on medication. My sister is still protected, but probably will be headed there in the near future. My mother was one of the last to have arthritis of the hip. She didn't start school until fourth grade because she was ill. We always valued health in our family.

After the first four months of being in the program, all of the health-related numbers improved. Then, on test number three, my triglycerides went from a 207 to 295. The third quarter they went to 472. At the end of the program, my cholesterol was 219 and my triglycerides kept going up. I substituted all meat for pasta. Now they tell me that my body changes pasta into sugar, so my diet is constantly changing. I am trying to find substitutes for meat and lowering carbohydrates. I also have a high metabolism and was losing weight. I didn't want to lose weight.
(Caution — See statement at the end of this story)

I was committed to this group and the program for a year. My support structure was the group. My wife and family can eat all the junk they want and not gain weight or increase their cholesterol, so they don't want to change their behavior. My wife eats what she wants for dinner, and I eat what I want.

I would talk to others in the program, and it was working for all of us. Sometimes I will on a holiday or something, go off the diet; but 85-90 percent of the time I do stick to it. Travel is a barrier. It is hard, but if I have to go off the diet, I eat pasta or fish. So, even when I go off the diet I eat healthy. I will always find a restaurant that will prepare the entrees the way I prefer them.

I only attempted to change this behavior one time. I've started on it, have stuck with it and haven't changed other behaviors. I've always eaten healthy. Now, I do read labels because you have to be careful and see what is in the food.

I didn't have a role model; I just went along with the group. Motivation for making the change was my cholesterol shooting up with no change in exercise and diet. The group held monthly sessions to discuss food, go to the grocery store, and modify recipes. They made it fun because it is not easy. If it were easy, everyone would be doing it. I am not on medication, but I continue to monitor my cholesterol and triglyceride numbers. We've been doing this for two years and we keep trying. I was prepared for the change as much as you can be for "cold turkey".

Looking back on it, I wouldn't do anything differently. I just had to commit and not go into it half way. I won't have trouble maintaining the change, but it is difficult because of the battle with triglycerides; someone give me a break from the heredity!

Caution: In an effort to allow each interviewee to tell his or her own story, all statements made were left unchanged. Most diet experts recommend a balanced diet, eating a variety of healthy foods. For more information on the diet that is right for you, consult a registered dietician or your physician.

Leona H.

32-Year-Old Female

Oakland, CA/Houston, TX

Weight Loss

Overcoming Depression

I was born in Oakland, California and now live in Houston, Texas. I am 32 years-old, single and female. I have a Bachelor's degree in Business Administration.

Until recently, I had been overweight since the time I was a toddler. When I was 11-years-old, my grandmother passed away. She was the main caretaker for my brother and I. So when she passed away, my brother and I became responsible for each other. I began to spend a lot of time focusing on food and watching television as a way of coping, rather than going outside and playing. It replaced an emptiness that I felt. That continued over time. I had been overweight before, but the feelings from her death led to an increase in my weight. I ended up on several diets off-and-on, and tried numerous things in an attempt to control my weight.

Something that finally worked was the *Weigh Down Workshop*, (see reference in Appendix C) which is a Christian-based program where the goal is to remove the focus from yourself and the things used to fulfill you. The program instructs you to place the focus on God instead. It is a national and worldwide program held at different churches or peoples' homes. Through the workshop, I have lost 150 lbs. in the past year. The program is more than just about weight loss; it's about the underlying things. I feel we have a tendency to run to material things, rather than God. Prior to these workshops, going to church was just a ritual. I just went on Sundays because I felt it was something I was supposed to do.

When I was 11, and my grandmother was my primary caregiver, my home environment was different in terms of diet and exercise. My health environment was probably a bit more controlled. She was the one person that really gave me a good foundation; to go to church, be a good person, etc. In terms of eating, it was better controlled because there was someone taking care of me, rather than me looking for something to fill that emptiness.

Controlling how many fat grams, calories, and what types of food I was eating, or my level of exercise didn't do a bit of good — I needed to change my heart.

Growing up I went through a number of continuous cycles. That was the only way I knew how to handle life. I was depressed. I wasn't on medication; I had gone to see counselors, but it didn't help. I would end up continuing to overeat, so nothing was working until I was introduced to this program. I've seen religious and non-religious counselors, and even had one person tell me that I could have been on medication for my depression, but I'm thankful that I didn't turn to that. My depression is no longer an issue.

Past jobs never really affected my lifestyle. In my current company, it's affected my lifestyle in a good way because they've allowed me to enroll in wellness classes at work. After work, I meet people with my same weight-loss goal, and that's been critical to my success. **I don't feel it is typical that companies offer programs like this, but I feel it is critical that these classes be made available to employees as they provide a supportive environment for co-workers.**

In terms of going through phases, for me, it was finally realizing that I had to change my heart. **Controlling how many fat grams, calories, and**

what types of food I was eating, or my level of exercise didn't do a bit of good — I needed to change my heart. When I finally understood this, with the help of the program, I was finally able to see that God was calling me to be totally obedient in all areas of my life. Prior, I was being disobedient by overeating and eating when I wasn't really hungry. Once I understood that, I had such joy, peace and happiness knowing that I'm doing His will. He has continued to refine me and show me different areas that I need to improve — like maybe watching too much television. For someone else it may be exercising too much. Another area of support for me was seeking praise from other people. I've never been as happy as I am now. I weigh the same as I did when I was an 11 or 12-year-old, which is very sad. I know that He (God) is going to take more weight, and I know it's not going to come back.

When I first began my health behavior change, I didn't really want to set a goal. I just thought, "Well I've tried everything else, I might as well just try this." But, as I've continued, I have a goal in mind. It's changed from looking at the weight to looking at my heart. My goal has been to be totally obedient to what God is calling me to do, and that is to not live for me but to live for what He wants. That's what our purpose here on this earth is. It's not for our own good, but for His — to make Him look good and make Him happy.

My support over time, changed, after joining the *Weigh Down Workshop*. I felt guided to leave the church I was in and join another church fellowship. In my new church, I feel we're all on that same path. My church wants to be totally obedient to God, and to do that, we need to let go of focusing on ourselves and focus on God's will. The members are not going to just pat you on the back and say it's OK when it's really not. The people in church help encourage you to do what is needed. Changing churches was my key environmental change, because when I made that change, the weight basically fell off.

The biggest barrier I faced during my health behavior change was me. I had tried to control my eating behavior my entire life. I then asked for His guidance, rather than trying to control it by dieting or anything else. I did experience one relapse. I began suffering from depression again. I was never formally diagnosed or prescribed medication, but comparing my life to what it was before, the difference is like night and day.

My role model has been, and is now, Christ. He went through so much; how he actually lived his life, and lived within God's boundaries — I feel He is the ultimate example and role model.

At first, my motivation was just to lose weight and feel better so people would look at me more positively, and not treat me differently. Now though, my motivation is that I want to be obedient to God. I know that if I'm not, what's at risk is my salvation. If I'm not going to be obedient here on earth; if I'm going to be greedy and grab things that He has not giving me, then why would he want me in heaven?

For support materials, I only used the materials in the *Weigh Down Workshop*, which are all scripture-based. When I was younger, I used Dexatrim and things like that. For depression, the way I would cope was to come home after work, sit on the couch, watch television, and eat.

For this last weight-loss attempt, I feel I was completely equipped and prepared to make this change by changing churches and receiving the support needed.

If I had to do it again, I'd change my surroundings a lot quicker. It was such a key element for me to leave my current surroundings and re-evaluate everything that was in my life. I would have changed a lot quicker if I knew then, what I know now. It wouldn't have taken me this third time to finally get it right. I don't think I will have trouble maintaining this change in the future because it's not about the external; it's about my heart, and my heart has changed. I've learned that when you take something away, you need to fill it with what you need. In this case, and in all cases, you should be filling everything with God. I know people that have quit smoking and have turned to God to fill that emptiness. That's what has made the difference for me, and I know that I'm not going to go back. I think I am the "Reformer" personality type.

The best advice I can give is to seek God first, and allow Him to fill the emptiness you feel in your heart. No matter how much we try to fill the emptiness with material things, the only thing that can fill us is God. The program I went through is an awesome lesson in mere Christianity. That's all it is. They're not pointing you to a specific person. They're pointing you back to God, and what it says in the scripture.

Brian C. (sic)

25-Year-Old Male

Canterbury, NH

Weight Loss

My name is Brian C. I am 25 years-old, single and male from Canterbury, New Hampshire. I have a Bachelor's degree in architecture from the University of Cincinnati. The behavior change that I successfully achieved is weight loss. Let me just say the weight loss we're talking about was from a peak weight of about 238 pounds to 195-190 now, depending on the season. I lost all of that weight in about a year and I've kept it off for about 4 years now.

My mother is an Occupational Health Nurse now, but she's always been a nurse. At one point her job was Director of Community Education, so it was her job to teach people how to take care of their bodies. She always taught my two older sisters and I how to take care of our bodies. Unfortunately, I probably neglected her lessons more so than my sisters. I was slightly overweight ever since age 11 or 12. In college I had all of the bad health habits that college kids have, like eating a lot of junk food and drinking beer. I began putting on far more weight in college than I did when I was a teen. I became obese. My mom pointed this out to me, as well as other people in my life. I knew that it was unhealthy, so I would say just having my mom around during my upbringing was certainly a portion of my life that contributed to my lifestyle change.

I was in my fifth year of college, and I knew that I was too heavy. I didn't like it very much. Me and another friend of mine from my hometown in Wauseon bet each other $100 to see who could lose the most weight in a year. We both lost 40 pounds, so then it was double or nothing. We bet to see who could keep it off for the next year. We both kept it off for about a year. I just stopped keeping beer in my refrigerator; I stopped eating fast food, and started eating less in general. So, in a nutshell it was my mom's words of advice when I was growing up really, that added to it. Don't eat a lot because people in the United States, generally eat too much. Also, I don't drink a lot of beer like other college kids do; It'll make you pudgy. Moderation was the key to my weight loss.

When people say you look good, it tends to help you feel good, too.

Growing up in my home I had good portion sizes and was well feed. But it was once again around age 13 or so that I began to eat more independently, and that was because I actually worked. During the summers I worked full time, so I was eating a couple of meals by myself or with the crew that I was working with.

In terms of motivation, I knew I was getting too heavy. I didn't like the way that I looked. I was certainly not satisfied with my self-image, and my self confidence was also an issue. I knew it was unhealthy. I was unhealthy psychologically and physically.

Everyone supported me; my family, college friends, extended family, and relatives as well. Once they started to recognize I was losing weight, of course they all started saying "Wow, you're loosing some weight!" I said "yes," and they'd say "you look good!" Then I'd say, "Hey, I feel good!" **When people say you look good, it tends to help you feel good, too.** So it all just added to it. I'd say everyone who was a close relation supported me because they could all recognize that something like losing weight and achieving good health is a positive change for me.

I'm laid back, driven and an achiever. I am laid back in the sense that not too many things really stress me very much. But, when I recognize something of importance I generally pursue it. I go after a lot of things that I think are of positive quality or of high value. These personality traits helped me lose weight.

I actually kept most of my recreational habits, and my friends, because I recognized those were a positive part of my life. The major changes were with my personal habits. I kept a lot of the high fat, high salt out of my kitchen and bought more fruits and vegetables. It was a constant change when I would go shopping. I would know what I had around the house. When I went out with friends, I kept the good habits.

I didn't have any barriers that I know of. I modified my behavior, knowing that if I stuck with it I would have the results that I wanted.

I'm in the process right now of going through the same sort of physiological undertaking. I have recently been told by my doctor that I have borderline blood pressure. I'm realizing that I've got to change other behaviors now; to exercise more, watch salt intake, etc.

I didn't really have a role model. I knew the behavior pattern that I had to obtain, so I just followed that as opposed to a role model.

I had a lifetime of my mother instructing me as to what good eating habits were and how to moderate not-so-good eating habits. It was simply applying the guidelines that I had been taught during my childhood and not ignoring them for a change. I wouldn't do anything differently, and I don't think I will have any trouble maintaining this behavior change in the future.

If you eat too much you're going to weigh too much. If you eat less, you'll probably weigh less. It's a really simple formula; you just need to make it a part of you're lifestyle, as opposed to just some words in a book. It has to be more than an idea, it's your behavior.

Jeanne G.

59-Year-Old Female
Nebraska
Increased Physical Activity
Weight Loss

I am 59 years-old married and female, with three children. I spent most of my childhood in Nebraska, where I was one of five children raised in a low-socioeconomic upbringing. I am currently middle-class, and I work with customer information databases.

I increased my physical activity, and lost 47 pounds over a 13 month period. A "successful" change to me is setting the goals, maintaining the change, and sticking with it. I made this behavior change 13 months ago. I had previously, and unsuccessfully, attempted to change my health behavior of increasing my physical activity four times.

I felt I did go through various stages. I felt good, then I would question if I was doing a good job because the weight was not falling off fast enough.

The original motivation for making this change was that I wanted to prevent the family trend of "being big". My aerobics instructor provided support for this change, but I relied mostly on myself to make this change. I didn't receive a lot of support from the people in my life. I also used written materials and some professional help. My physician knows about my change and was very supportive. Once your doctor compliments you, you want to do even better. I do not have a role model, or anyone who gave me inspiration.

The recommendation that I would give to others is that everyone is capable of changing. **Look at it as healthy eating, not dieting.**

Set reasonable goals and go for it. If you feel like you are falling back, then talk with someone that will push you; we are all human.

The personality type that best fits me is the "Challenger". I set out to do it — so I was going to accomplish it. I was determined.

My main source of motivation was that I wanted to feel better and better. I thought to myself, "I can do it." When I originally set my goals I was unsure how prepared I was. The change occurred because of timing. I had to do it right then and there. The time was perfect as I felt like there was, no time like the present. If I were to do it again, I wouldn't do anything differently. The one thing that was crucial to my success was getting a totally different attitude and mind set.

Roger P. (sic)

60-Year-Old Male
Brooklyn, NY/Omaha, NE
Weight Loss
Increased Physical Activity

I am 60 years-old, married and male. I was born, and grew up in Brooklyn, New York. I now live in Omaha, Nebraska. I have two college degrees.

Over the last two years I've lost both my parents. My mother died of congestive heart failure. She had heart problems, diabetes, and high blood pressure. It was all due to being overweight. I watched her for years, trying to control her weight, and she was never able to do that successfully. On my father's side, his brother, father, and grandfather have died from heart attacks. I look back on it all now, and diet had a lot to do with it. During my upbringing, we ate a lot of very fat foods. We cooked our foods in lard. I always had a weight problem, even when I was in school. I would vary from being overweight to being at a normal weight all the time, depending on the activities I was involved in. **When I was doing activities I would lose weight, and when I would stop the activities I would gain weight. I never really connected my diet to that problem until years later.**

I was concerned about my health all of my life. But, after burying my parents I said, "You know, I don't have any of the symptoms, I don't have high blood pressure, I don't have diabetes, and my heart is in good shape." I had been running on the treadmill up until just about the time my parents died. However, I said, "Well I'm not happy, and I'm going to escape all that stuff." Then, in the last few years, I started to get the symptoms; I was getting overweight, and I was getting pains in my legs and my joints. Along with arthritis and high blood pressure, I started having breathing problems and I would get pains in my chest.

I was concerned with the symptoms that I started to have. Then, I started worrying about diabetes. I said, "I have to do something about this." Then my wife, God bless her, indicated that people at work were doing Weight Watchers. She encouraged me to join. I said, "I don't need that, I can do this on my own." So, I tried the Atkins diet, and I tried Heart

---

When I was doing activities I would lose weight, and when I would stop the activities I would gain weight. I never really connected my diet to that problem until years later.

Healthy diets. I never could lose weight, permanently. I would lose 10 or 20 pounds, but then I would gain it right back because I couldn't follow the diet very well. I probably wasn't motivated, or what I was trying to do on my own was not sufficient. Then, my kids started complaining that I was getting overweight and having health problems. My grandkids would say, "Grandpa why are you so fat?" So, I said, "You know, I've got to do something about this!" Right about then, probably at just the right time, when I was in the right mood, I got a flyer that indicated there was a Weight Watchers at Work (see reference in Appendix C) program at my job. Of course, I heard about it before from my wife. So, I decided to give it a try. At the same time, the wellness center at my job offered two other programs, *Weight-No-More* (see reference in Appendix C) and Nutrition-For-You (see reference in Appendix C). I took advantage of those as well. Another behavior change was that I increased my exercise to at least three times a week. I tried to do it religiously. I was participating in an exercise class at work. I started walking, and still walk about 2.5 miles a day in the gym. I decided, "You know, all of this is not that bad, I can deal with this."

All of this started occurring around November of 2001. I wanted to lose

100 pounds in a year; that was my goal. I had this focus in my mind. So, I had to have something out there as a goal to achieve, and weekly weigh-ins for Weight Watchers was another motivating factor. I didn't want to fail. Failure to me was gaining weight. **There were days when I would say, "I don't want to do this stuff anymore." My wife kept me on track. If there was one person in my life that helped me during this time, it was my wife. I don't think I could have done it without her.**

I would get discouraged at times because I didn't lose as much weight as I wanted, and the other thing that helped me was the counselors at Weight Watchers. They have been through this with a lot of people before, so they would support me by saying, "Don't get discouraged, keep at it, the weight will come off." Also, their motivational speeches at the weekly meetings were very helpful. This is where I learned about portion control.

From then on, I was very diligent in my portion control, and in making sure I ate only what I needed to eat. Before, I was always concerned that I wouldn't get enough nutrients if I didn't get large quantities of food. One thing I like about the Weight Watchers diet is the flexibility. I like steak and potatoes, and I still eat that today. However, I eat those things in the right portions, and in moderation. There are no forbidden foods with this program, so all I had to do was eat according to the point system. I find that very easy to do, rather than counting calories, carbohydrates and proteins. Of all the diets out there, this is the one I have never worried about. I keep within the point totals. I learned from the *Nutrient-For-You* program, how it all works and I said, "Jeez, the Weight Watchers diet provides for all the nutrients that you need." So, I wasn't concerned about being nutrient deprived. The other diets I tried, with the way they were structured, you only eat certain foods. I didn't have a variety of fruits in my diet since they were banned because of the carbohydrate content. So, Weight Watchers is what worked for me, and I have been doing it ever since.

I have actually lost 101 pounds. After I lost the weight my wife was looking through some old pictures from Christmas back in 2000, 2001, and 2002. I could not believe the difference. It didn't even look like me; I had to look twice to be sure it was me in the pictures. Now, I carry one of those pictures with me, and I look at it periodically. I say to myself, "I'm never going back to that weight."

I don't think my actual job did anything to promote my behavior changes. My job is a sedentary one; I just sit. So, my job doesn't contribute to what I do physically. Actually, it is the other way around. **I think losing the weight has affected the way I do my job now. Now I have better stamina; I can get more things done in a day. I used to get tired. I think I bring more to the job now because of my energy, and alertness. I do feel more alert.**

Another thing that's kind of peculiar is, about a couple of years ago, I was being kind of forgetful. We would make a joke of it, saying it was old age or Alzheimer's. We were making fun of it, but I've noticed lately I have a better memory. I don't know if it's all related, but that is another thing I noticed; I don't forget as much as I used to.

Another thing that has changed is that I used to hate yard work. Now I'm into yard work. **I used to go outside and only do 10 minutes of work before I was exhausted. Now I can go out there for as long as I want and I don't get tired — I just have more energy; more ability to do things. My joints don't hurt anymore, and I just feel a whole lot better. I feel as if I were 20 years younger.** In fact twenty years ago was when I retired from the Air Force. I am 16 pounds lighter now, than I was when I left the Air Force. It is great because everybody, my children and grandchildren, feel that they are going to have their father or grandfather around a little longer now.

As far as running into barriers or experiencing relapse, like I said, I just allocated my points appropriately according to the Weight Watchers plan.

I would eat more than I should at Thanksgiving, or at a party, but I planned for that. The only barrier I have is temptation. I go to these places and the food is plentiful. I am tempted, but I stick to the diet. I know what I should eat. I avoid the things I shouldn't eat. I take my partner with me, my wife, and she reminds me, "You shouldn't have that, don't look at that." She watches over me.

We made small adjustments at home, in what we eat. I stay away from the prime rib, but my wife eats the prime rib; I eat fillets instead. It was the little changes. We used to eat spaghetti with meatballs and sausage; I don't eat as much as I did before. I keep my meals within portion control. Instead of eating two meatballs, I'll only have one. Instead of eating two cups of spaghetti, I'll have one. Instead of eating a half loaf of bread, I'll have just a one slice. It's all about portion control, rather than changing the entire diet. So, we really didn't change a whole lot. My wife was brought up in an Italian/German background, and they modified Mediterranean type diets. It involved lots of vegetables and meats, but like I said, it's all portion control. She didn't cook with fat, but I like my Polish food, so we would have Polish food only every once in a while. She would eat small portions of it; I would eat large portions of it. And now I avoid a lot of that. I eat that very sparingly now. The biggest key in losing weight and maintaining it is to watch what you eat, and the quantity of what you eat.

The personality type that I feel represents me is the "Reformer". Having this personality type helped me because one of the characteristics is that I am purposeful; I have a purpose out there. Also, I have self-control. I can control myself and I am a principled person. I don't think I'm a perfectionist. I do expect things to be done right, but I don't know if that makes me a perfectionist. I'm not obsessive about it. I'm idealistic too. I think, looking back, that's exactly what part of my success was; putting a goal out there and having self-control and a lot of help from my wife.

I did not have any role models through my behavior change. However, there was a backward role model. There was an individual that I was a friend with. He was overweight, and he had knee problems. I said to myself that I don't want to be like him. I could see that happening with me, because I was starting to get leg pains; he was huffing and puffing down the hallways, and I also was huffing and puffing. I was sitting there saying to myself, "I'm going in that direction." So, I told myself I didn't want to be like him. This was one thing I can look back on and say had a lot of influence on me. I thought about it as I entered the program, and it kept going through my mind. I still keep those images in my mind now, and I don't want to be that way.

I did use the Internet and other materials to help with my behavior change. Some of the best things were the stories that people shared. They were motivational. I would listen, or I would read the stories; particularly Weight Watchers, they have great stories. I would read the stories and say, "If they can do it, I can do it." Some of the people I read about had the same problems I had. They beat it, and I wanted to be like them as well. Not all the stories relate to me exactly, but there were elements of the stories that I could relate to. Every one of them had something positive that contributed to keeping my mind on track.

When I decided to make the change, I guess I didn't realize how drastic it was going to be from my previous diets, or how much it was going to cost me. In terms of clothes, I went from a size 46 down to a 36. As I kept losing weight I had to keep changing my wardrobe. I never thought about that part of weight loss, but it was kind of nice. I never thought of the dollars, in terms of clothing. So, I wasn't prepared for it. I would go through the closest and, I can't tell you how many thousands of dollars I've thrown out in clothes. I was losing weight so fast; I didn't realize losing a hundred pounds would make a clothes size difference. When I got clothes that were new, I would lose weight faster than I could wear them. I would just take the old clothes and donate them to the Goodwill.

If I had to do it again, what I would do differently is I would have started a lot sooner. I would have started an exercise program earlier, and been committed to that. That's the only thing I would change. It took me 5 or 6 months to get into an exercise program. I should have done it earlier, much earlier.

One thing that is interesting, and a big reason I exercise is, the convenience of having a place at work. If it weren't for the convenience, I don't know if I would do that. I think the convenience of having an exercise facility at work is a tremendous boost for me. I exercise a lot after work now. Before, I would go home, and once I get home I would say to myself, "I'm finished for the day." Now, I leave work and I go right by the gym. I say, "Gee, it's only 30 or 45 minutes, I can spend that time in there and I still get home at a decent hour." Now when I get home, I don't have to worry about changing clothes and going back out to the gym. I just go right there, right at work. It's very convenient. I thank my employer for having that. It is such an asset to the company. I don't know how many people participate, but it is a valuable tool for me.

I don't think I will have any problem maintaining my behavior change in the future. I'm still motivated to keep the weight off; I don't think I'll have any problem. Many people, including myself, with a small child or grandchild, realize our hours in this life are limited.

My advice for others who would want to make the changes I made is, believe that you can do it. Keep believing, and don't ever give up. If you have a relapse or discouragement pick yourself up, dust yourself off, and get on with it. It's only one day out of a lifetime. You've got to think about this as a lifetime change. The day you fail is only one

day out of a lot of other good days throughout the rest of your life. So, keep yourself motivated and you can do it.

Tracy A. (sic)

32-Year-Old Female
Fridley, MN/Washington, DC
Weight Loss

I was born in Fridley, Minnesota and now live in the Washington, D.C. metro area. I am 32 years-old single and female with a master's degree.

I grew up in Minnesota and other parts of the Midwest. My parents divorced when I was about eight years old. I lived with my mother, except for one year when I lived with my dad.

I lost 120 pounds through regular exercise. Losing weight was something that I had been trying to do for most of my life. It all started about three years ago when I moved to Washington. I went on a business trip to Hawaii and felt out of place. Everyone was snorkeling and doing outdoors stuff, and I stayed in the hotel room. That episode had a big impact on me and galvanized me into action. It was shortly after that trip when I decided I was fed up, and I had to do things differently. It all came together. My job involved a lot of travel and I was just thinking that my weight was only going to get worse unless I did something about it. My career is not going to go the way I want it to if I am not able to travel and socialize.

Growing up, I lived mostly with my mom in a single-parent home. Having to work, she was not home a lot. So, I was left to prepare the meals for my brother and myself. Because I was so young, I prepared a lot of pre-packaged foods. My mother just wanted to make sure we had food, so there was no real monitoring of serving sizes or nutrition. My mother was a permissive parent, so there were not really a lot of strict rules concerning eating habits. She kept food around to make sure we were pacified.

During my life, except for the one year that I lived with my dad, I was always overweight. In fifth grade, while living with my dad, I lost about 30 pounds. It was something he was interested in. He had been heavy as a child and lost weight. Unfortunately, I did it for him and not for myself. When you are in fifth grade, you do as you're told. So as soon as I moved out of that environment, I gained all the weight back, and then some.

Since I made the decision two and a half years ago, I have been tenacious about sticking with it. I have never strayed off the path. Once I made up my mind, I just did it. The night that I made the decision, I spoke to my dad on the phone. He has been my coach through all of this and we talk weekly. I talked to him on the phone that night and told him that I really wanted to lose weight and I was committed to it. He had heard that before, so even though he was supportive I was not sure he really thought I would go through with it. But after I got off the phone I went and threw away all of the food in my house. I think that was a necessary, cathartic experience for me. Next, I went to the store and bought all new food. I had just read the book by Dean Ornish — Eat More Weigh Less, and I found it to be very inspiring. I tried to base my decisions on the recommendations in that book.

When I started I was very militant about my food. I made all of my own food and I followed a lot of the recipes in his book. Since then, I have gone through a stage to loosen up a little bit on the diet. It's hard to be social when you have such a restricted diet, so I have made modifications. I have lost most of the weight I intended, except for this last pesky 10 pounds.

I have used *Weight Watchers* in the past. I have also tried almost all other weight loss programs. I thought they were all fine, but they just did not work well for me. I am not the type of person who needs a group environment like *Weight Watchers*. I did use the Internet for some information. However, if I am interested in a particular food, especially when I am going out to eat with friends, I try to get calorie and nutrient information before I go. There is a website called *Nutri-size* that provides some basic diet and exercise information. I am on their newsletter mailing list. I also use exercise videos for my workouts. There is also a website called *Video Fitness*. I use their reviews to choose my workouts.

I have been in pretty good control except for a very short period when I decided to be defiant and intentionally not address my weight. I went through a period when I said that I was just going to be happy with myself and forget trying to change. I would say, "I am just going to live with myself the way I am." That lasted for about six months and I gained a lot of weight, so it wasn't a good attitude to have. I think my most recent problem, and this has been my main barrier, is trying to balance social activities and eating. Unfortunately, a big part of socializing is eating. I keep trying to think of other things I can do, but it always comes back to eating first and then doing other things. So, trying to find a balance has been real difficult, and I am still struggling with that.

Once I made this serious attempt I never had a significant relapse. The first two years I didn't gain any weight over the holidays. But, in the years that followed I would gain a couple of pounds over the holidays; partly because of my relaxing of the food restrictions. I lost the weight again, so I don't really consider it a relapse.

I know I will not have a problem maintaining the change in the future, partly because I have become an exercise addict. Now I am very rigorous about my fitness. So, when I do have vacations and holidays where I eat more, it is usually balanced by my working out. During my serious attempt to lose weight, I did both exercise and caloric restriction concurrently. This is because I have always been a big believer that weight loss without exercise just doesn't work very well. Also, I just wanted to be healthier.

My dad was definitely one of my role models. I remember when I was a kid, my dad went out and started running one night around the block and that then motivated him to eventually do a marathon. That is so inspiring. Also, this may sound crazy but I read this book by Oprah Winfrey and her trainer, called *Making the Connection*. For some reason the words really inspired me. She was talking about an experience with the Emmys' where she didn't want to win because she didn't want to have to go on stage. That just struck me because I understood that feeling of wanting to hide in the audience.

I have been inspired by other people's success stories too. I think it is helpful to have other people to relate to. The personality types I feel most connected with are the "Reformer", and "Achiever", and the "Investigator". The characteristic I have from both the "Reformer" and the "Achiever" is I am a driven, goal-oriented person. Being that way definitely helped me. Plus, I am extremely stubborn. Although the one question I can't answer is, what separated my success this time from the other times? I think being tenacious, goal-oriented, and image-conscious helped. This is especially true here in D.C. where there is definitely a young professional crowd.

Maybe that is what the difference was when I made my behavior change this time. I was living here in D.C. and this environment may have pushed me over the top. I tend to be a loner and not group-oriented. I know a lot of people have success with programs where groups are involved. Maybe being more of a loner has hindered me in the past because I am not getting as much social support. I don't know whether it has or not.

I did not use any medications, over the counter or prescribed. I felt prepared to make this behavior change in that I knew exactly what I needed to do. For a long time, I have known what I needed to do.

In my view, weight loss is fairly simple. You need to burn more calories than you consume and you will lose weight. That is the bottom line! I felt very prepared. I've studied it all my life. I consider myself an expert on weight loss. I just needed to put my knowledge into action and I felt confident that I could. I was surprised by my ability to keep going for so long.

I would not do anything differently if I had it to do again. The advice that I would give to others is to be as stubborn as possible because you don't see outstanding results in the first two weeks. You have to stick with it and you will see results in the longer term. But I think a lot of people try something and if by week two they haven't seen a major loss they say, "Well this isn't working." My first week I think I only lost 1/2 pound. I was really disappointed, and it took two or three weeks until I saw bigger losses. Before that, I definitely had thoughts of giving up. That was my past experience too, so I would like to convey to people to stick with it although I know that it is not very original.

Other advice I would give is that the exercise portion goes hand-in-hand with the nutrition side. I started with very simple workouts, nothing that involved jumping around or anything. With my weight, I couldn't have done any of that. I never liked exercising and it was a real struggle. I did it at 5:00 in the morning, six days a week. I wanted to do it before work because I knew that if I would try to do it later in the day, I would find a reason not to. I think that was the general key for me. I use videos, which also helped because then I didn't have to go to the health club and be seen by other people.

I read that it takes about six weeks to form a habit, so just keep exercising for that long and you will be hooked. It took longer than six weeks for me. I didn't think I would ever be hooked, but eventually I was. It took about six months before I wanted more challenging workouts. That opened a new door for me where I wanted to challenge myself physically. I have really diversified my workouts since then. During the first six weeks, I was too heavy to enjoy it.

I started to see muscles, definition and things that I was never able to see before. I thought, "Wow, this is great!" I did *Tae Bo* with my dad. He has been such a huge influence on me and he couldn't keep up. It was a really big moment for me. The fact that he was impressed meant a lot.

It is uncountable how many times I tried to lose weight in the past. For me, weight loss has changed my life in so many ways and the positive effects just keep multiplying over time.

It is uncountable how many times I tried to lose weight in the past. For me, weight loss has changed my life in so many ways and the positive effects just keep multiplying over time. I received a lot of reinforcement. Not only were people being supportive, but also you start feeling better in general. You have more energy, you are able to buy new, smaller clothes and fit into airplane seats. It just never ends. You get constant positive reinforcement.

The one thing that I would tell people I have discovered about exercising is that no matter how crappy you feel and how much you don't want to workout — do it. There has never been a single time in the last 2 1/2 years where I have regretted doing it once I got started. There are those days where you just say, "I can't do this, I am tired, I feel yucky, I'd just rather watch TV..." But, if you force yourself to do it, you will always be glad you did!

Steven B. (sic)

35-Year-Old Male
Southwestern Iowa
Weight Loss
Increased Physical Activity

I am 35 years-old and male. I grew up in southwest Iowa, and have no children.

My family had been big eaters all my life. We were a farm family, and I didn't necessarily eat bad things, but ate big meals. I have been big all of my life. I weighed 90 pounds in kindergarten. **I knew that I had to change my lifestyle. I didn't want to go on any fad diets or eat any special foods, I just wanted to eat healthy and do something I could continue for the rest of my life.** It may sound corny, but I don't live to eat anymore; I eat to live, and I'm a big eater who loves to eat. I did it by just changing my focus, really. I look at food differently now. I still really love food and like to cook, but I just eat healthier foods and am not on any special diets. I write down everything I eat, everyday. That was one of the behaviors I had to change, I had to think about everything I ate. **Sometimes I fell off my plan and ate something that I wanted for one meal or for even a whole day, and if I did fall off the plan, I did not let it discourage me. I went right back on my routine.** I exercise regularly by keeping focused and making myself work out. With exercise, I also tried not to be too hard on myself. If something came up and I was unable to exercise that day, I wouldn't worry about it. I would say to myself, "It is only one day." **I started by changing what I was eating first, and then added exercise three months later. I started walking 15-20 minutes every day, worked up to 45 minutes, and then an hour. I started lifting weights and got into Tae Kwon Do. I became healthier, in better shape, and it got easier.**

Prior to this health behavior change, I had made only two attempts to change throughout my entire life. Once in college (1989), trying the same approach, but I was probably too hard or restrictive on myself. And one other time I changed my behavior for a couple of months and lost 10 pounds, but that didn't last either.

I had some barriers, but not many, because I was so focused. At work, there can be a lot of food. I had to realize that just because there is food there, I don't have to eat it. Also, moderation is important. I can plan my meals and bring my lunch, but food always pops up. Moderation is the key, so I can have one cookie or one bite of something. Sometimes, just having a taste is all I need.

I also ran into barriers with my weight loss. On average, I lost a couple of pounds a week, and then hit a plateau which was hard and discouraging. Sometimes, on a weekend, I would eat whatever I wanted. Sometimes that would work and I would get right back on my diet, but it also affected my metabolism. It took me three to four weeks to get into a diet routine. I got into the habit of counting calories. As I lost weight and became healthier, exercise became easier, more fun, and not a chore. I needed to be challenged. I enjoyed seeing the physical changes of my appearance; seeing the weight drop off. Wal-Mart became my friend for clothes. I am not spending a lot on my current clothes, because I hope that I will not be in them too much longer. My starting weight was 360, and I'm now at 185-190 pounds. I lost 175 pounds. My freshman year of high school I weighed 200-240.

I have a great family (many who have to watch their weight as well) who were very supportive. Friends and co-workers were most supportive. Some co-workers who really didn't know me would ask, "Have you lost a lot of weight?" While in line at the cafeteria, food service people would comment "You have lost a lot of weight!" The same people would comment, again, that I looked like I was still losing weight. There were days I would weigh myself at work, and it seemed I hadn't lost any weight. When I was a little discouraged, it seemed that these were the times when I would walk down the hall and someone would make a positive comment. I would use that as motivation; my family and friends being supportive and encouraging.

I did not use any materials to assist me with this change. My mother and sister-in-law are nurses, while my brother and his wife are doctors. I told them what I was doing and they all signed off on it. I played sports in high school and lifted weights, so I knew what I had to do. I am stubborn and don't like someone telling me what to do.

I was always told that I needed to lose weight. I saw my doctor about six years ago for heart problems and found out that I was having premature ventricular contractions, which is hereditary. I just didn't feel well, not sick, but not good. When I changed jobs, I decided to change routines. I decided to change it all. I worked better hours; the previous department was always keeping food available to make people happy. The change of environment, with less stress and less food helped. I had more time to focus on myself. I then saw my doctor one year ago, and I had lost ninety pounds. That was the first time I had seen my doctor in a while, and I thought he was going to kiss me. He walked into the room with a big grin on his face and said, "WOW! What have you been doing?!" All of the staff was concerned, but I told them that I had been exercising and eating healthier; they were impressed and felt I was doing great. They encouraged me to continue improving. I need to go back again and show them the weight I have lost since that time.

People always ask me what diet I am on. I tell them I count calories, eat right and exercise. You can see the look on their face, which seems to say, "Oh, crap." They seem to be hoping it is a pill. I knew this was a life-long challenge, and I think some people aren't up to doing what it takes. **It was difficult, but once I got into a routine; it wasn't. I guess I discovered I could eat things I wanted and stopped thinking, "Oh, I'll never be able to eat cake again." It's not true. Moderation is the key**.

I will have no problem keeping the weight off because it is now my lifestyle. To think of going back to what I was before is not an option. I told myself that would never happen. My goal is to weigh myself once a week or maybe every-other-week, then it won't be an obsession. I can keep myself in check. I'm not worried.

My motivation is that I want to be healthier, and have a better quality of life. I did not need a role model. I am making these changes for myself.

A recommendation to others is to start slow and set small, incremental goals. I didn't weigh myself for the first three months. I didn't want to know what I weighed. I just wanted to change my habits. I didn't want the pressure of losing weight at first. I lost almost 30 pounds before I had even weighed myself. Also, if you fall off one day, don't worry about it. Just get back on the next day. **Start slow and don't overdo it. The first time I was too hard on myself, and that didn't work.**

E. Dewey S.

75-Year-Old Male
Omaha, NE
Quit Smoking
Overcoming Alcohol Addiction
Increased Physical Activity

I was born and currently live in Omaha, Nebraska. I am 75 years-old male and have been married for 45 years.

I started smoking while in high school, when I was 15 years old. I used to go in the under-dwelling of the building to smoke. I joined the Marines after high school and was stationed on a ship, where I continued to smoke and also started drinking. Both alcohol and tobacco were very inexpensive. For example, a carton of cigarettes aboard ship, once at sea was $.70 cents. At that time in the military, physical activity was not very strenuous or emphasized. Up until 1946 my major activity was golf.

After the military, I returned home and went to the University of Nebraska for my Bachelors in Business Administration. My friends were now in post-graduate programs, studying medicine and law. I would spend Fridays drinking and smoking with them. My weight during college went up to 210 pounds. At the age of 29, I got married and began working at a savings and loan institution. Back then, a lot of socializing went on in this business. There were trade organization functions where there was a lot of partying, smoking, and drinking. I continued to drink fairly heavily. In fact, I was in the habit of having at least a martini a night, which caused problems between my wife and I. She began to bother me about my drinking. She believed that I was an alcoholic, because a psychiatrist had once told her that anyone who drank every day was an alcoholic.

There was one specific business trip where this all changed. A friend and I went to Phoenix and drank a lot during a three-day business trip. On the way home, I decided to have a beer on the plane however, this time I told my friend that it would be my last. That was February 1, 1975. I did not have another drink from that point on. This was the same year I purchased my first bike as an adult. I think it was a three speed. My two kids, who were 10 and 12 years old, were also interested in biking so I purchased bikes for all of us. I began riding in the evenings to relieve tension and found that it replaced the relaxing effect I would get from my drinking.

One year later, on February 1, 1976 I said, "A year ago I quit drinking — I bet I could quit smoking too." So I quit cold turkey and never had another cigarette. After I quit smoking I started to run just a little. I eventually worked up to two miles. However, in 1977 there was an economic downturn and I was having trouble focusing on my job and making things work. I was offered early retirement in 1977 and took it. During my one year of unemployment, my wife put our name in at the new Jewish Community Center (JCC). I would go there once in a while to swim and play racquetball. As my year of unemployment continued, I found myself spending more time at the JCC and exercising. I even helped plan a triathlon series they were implementing. At this time, this was a new event for us, so I signed up for a few triathlons and did fairly well. At 50, I ran my first 10K race and finished in 50 minutes. Looking back, the running shoes were not yet very sophisticated and not that easy to run in. Like in a triathlon, I was frequently doing all three sports. I would run in the early morning and swim in the evenings on most days. I found this helped with the tension and relieved the pain in my joints. Then I would bike on the weekends.

Over the years, as I changed jobs, I found that exercising helped me cope with the stress and tension. While my jobs and duties changed, exercise was my one relative constant activity. In fact, I kept doing my

morning runs and found that regardless of how the day went — good or bad, I still felt like I accomplished something by getting my runs in first thing in the morning. The exercise gave me a sense of accomplishment that I did not get from work or from some of the jobs I had.

In one of my last jobs, I remember being asked what I would like in the new building and I told them, "a shower," because on some days I was supplementing my morning runs with one in the afternoon just to help cope with the tension. I found that with giving up my other habits of smoking and drinking — I had to replace them with something, and exercise seemed the natural choice. I also found that when I started working from home in my last job, it was easy to snack. The exercise helped to stabilize my weight.

Because I was not smoking and drinking, I had a new social outlet with exercising and competition. I found this gave me something to talk about and be proud of. I also felt like some of my co-workers who still had the old habits of smoking and drinking might have been a bit envious that they did not have this positive outlet.

I never had a role model for any of the changes, nor did I ever take any prescription or over-the-counter medication. I have been running in the early mornings for about 25 years. I quit racing when I was 63. I would consistently go up one minute a year. So once I finished my last race at age 63, in 63 minutes, I said to myself, "I am done racing, but I will still continue to exercise."

I find that as I get older it does become tougher to do what I've been doing. For example, at age 73 I was running 6 miles a day, now, at 75 I am down to around 4-4 1/2 miles per day. I am not sure how long I will be able to continue with the running, but I still swim about one mile on most days of the week. I plan to continue swimming; I don't see a problem in staying with that activity.

The exercise gave me a sense of accomplishment that I did not get from work or from some of the jobs I had.

For my personality type I am a "Challenger". I think my wife would agree, especially with the confrontational part.

My advice to others is to not make too many changes very quickly. For example, in looking back, I think I made too many changes at possibly the wrong time in my life. My ability to concentrate on all the things I had to do was affected by my drastic lifestyle changes. I might have done them at the wrong time in my life and also may have over compensated on the physical training at times, but again, it served as a coping mechanism for me. **For others, the key is to pick the right time in your life, focus on self-satisfaction and control.** I did feel that I was prepared to make the lifestyle changes in my life, and never did experience any serious relapses.

I have been retired since 1994, and have a set routine of running in the mornings and swimming in the evenings. Overall, I feel good and plan to stay with it for as long as I can.

Julie S.

39-Year-Old Female
Omaha, NE
Quit Smoking

I am 39 years-old, married and female with one child. I am a college graduate with a Master's degree, and I am currently working in the Communications field. I was raised in an upper class family in Omaha, Nebraska with three siblings. I now consider myself to be middle class.

The health behavior change I successfully succeeded in was quitting smoking. I have been a non-smoker for at least two years. For me, a "successful" change is to stop smoking entirely.

I made this change two years ago. I tried to change this behavior four times before I was finally successful.

I felt like I went through physical and emotional withdrawal, depression, anxiety, and finally acceptance. My motivation for making this change, initially, was pregnancy. After a brief relapse, following the birth of my daughter, I quit again. However, it was much harder this time. I initially quit cold-turkey, but used Nicorette gum the second time, which I found to be very helpful.

My spouse, family, and co-workers provided me with support for my change. I received a lot of support from all three groups. I relied on my spouse the most for support.

I did not use any written materials — the Internet or other media forms to assist with this behavior change. I didn't seek the professional help of a counselor, coach, expert, or personal trainer. My physician does know about my behavior change, but I can't say he was supportive or helpful. I didn't have a role model either. I don't think I will have trouble maintaining my behavior change in the future.

For people wanting to make a similar change, my recommendation is: To change a behavior you must want it for yourself, it can't be pressure-based from others.

The personality type that fits me best is the "Peacemaker". The conformist part of me made quitting smoking difficult. I didn't want to quit just because that's what I should do.

My source of motivation was my inner belief that not smoking is best for my daughter's future health.

I feel I was not very prepared for making this change. Timing was the primary reason for making the change when I did.

One thing that was crucial to my success in changing this behavior was maintaining focus on the end result, which was better health and being more productive in the long run.

Ernesto R. (sic)

36-Year-Old Male
Durango, Mexico/Omaha, NE
Quit Smoking

I was born in Durango, Mexico and I have attended some college. Now I am married with two children, and live in Omaha, Nebraska.

I started smoking when I was in high school. I started to hang around with some friends that liked to party. I always said I was never going to smoke, but somebody eventually talked me into it. I ended up smoking for about 17 years. I was smoking about a pack a week. When I got married, I did want to quit. I'd been married for 12 years and had wanted to quit for a long time, but couldn't. I went as long as three months without smoking, then came back to it again. I tried different ways to quit: I gradually began slowing down and reducing how much I smoked. I even stopped drinking because when I drank I would crave a cigarette. I tried not drinking and just couldn't do it. Somebody told me about a hypnotist, and I really wanted to stop, so I gave it a shot. It worked. Believe it or not, I hate cigarettes now because I just don't like smoke. That's why I wanted to do this interview; because it worked for me and I wanted to help others. I went into this (quitting cigarettes) with an open mind because I really did want to quit. That's the thing; you really, really must want to quit. I had to put some effort in it, too. **The reason I wanted to quit was for my kids. I didn't smoke in the house, but they would see me smoking and I didn't want them to smoke. If I was taking five years off my life, I'd rather have those five years to spend with them.** So, that was my greatest motivation to quit smoking.

Regarding maintaining the change in the future — no, no, no, I am not going to smoke anymore. For some reason, now, I just don't like it. It doesn't bother me to be with someone that smokes cigarettes; it just reminds me of the days I used to smoke and how much better I feel now.

When I was under hypnosis, I don't remember falling asleep — I was wide-awake. I had my eyes closed, and the hypnotist took me back to when I was young, before I started smoking. My father used to smoke, and I didn't really think about it. I really can't tell you that I hated smoking because my father smoked, so I don't know. The majority of the people I've worked with have all smoked, so I've always been surrounded by smoke. They were supportive when I was trying to quit and tried not to smoke in front of me. My wife has never smoked her entire life; she never liked it either. I still go to the same places I went to when I smoked. For example, I've gone to a bar, just to see if I could go there without smoking. It has worked. I don't crave it. I tried to quit smoking about five or six times in the past. When I tried quitting by myself, I gained a lot of weight. That's about the only change I noticed. At the time, I was also very moody and cranky. Now, I walk a lot and I ride my bicycle.

I knew I was ready to make the change to stop smoking, because I would catch myself with a cigarette in my hand and I was not even enjoying it anymore. I was tired of smoking. **My advice for somebody that is trying to quit is, "Don't just think about yourself; also think of the people around you."** I never smoked around my kids. I know a lot of people that smoke in the car with their kids, and that makes me angry. That's not right. Think about your kids and your spouse. My wife used to tell me that I smelled like an ashtray. You can't smell yourself. Now I can smell it (smoke), and my appetite is better. Food tastes better now. When I used to smoke, I couldn't smell things as well. A couple weeks ago, my brother-in-law came into town. He smokes a lot and I could smell the smoke on him. He didn't smoke in the house, but when he came inside I now know what my wife had been talking about. That's just another reason. I'd do it (quit) mainly for yourself, but think about everybody around you. The friends that I currently work with both smoke and are trying to quit. I told them about hypnosis, and they don't believe it — even though they see that I am not smoking. I wish there was something that I could say or do to change their mind. The hypnosis is only $140. They are pretty much in the same situation I was in. They want to quit for their kids, and their spouses are tired of them smoking — but I guess they are not ready to quit. A person has to really want to stop, because, otherwise, they can try hypnotherapy and it won't work.

Stopping smoking has also helped my productivity at work. I feel a lot better and have more energy. I walk a lot at work and remember when I had to take the elevator instead of the stairs. I can tell a difference now — I can take the stairs again without having to catch my breath. I am becoming a lot healthier.

Jean K.

37-Year-Old Female
Reading, PA/Indianapolis, IN
Quit Smoking

My name is Jean K. I was born in Redding, Pennsylvania and currently live in Indianapolis, Indiana. I am 37 years-old, married and female. I have a Bachelors of Arts in English.

I think I initially started smoking cigarettes for a thrill. I smoked my first cigarette in 7th grade. We bought a package of cigarettes from one of those machines, back when they still had them. My girlfriend and I smoked the whole package, then spent the next hour vomiting. I began smoking off and on every weekend for a couple months, then quit, because we were the "good kids" in the popular group. When I became a teenager, my father became very strict with me. I have two brothers, and they seemed to get the freedom that I didn't have. I developed early, and my father really cracked down on me to the point where I felt he was unfair. When I was fifteen I got a job as a lifeguard working with the popular "party crowd". That summer I started smoking regularly and continued smoking for the next 15 years. I was class President, on the basketball team and a three sport letter winner; so it was contradictory to be smoking and drinking. I felt like I was leading a double life. My issues with weight and cigarettes began simultaneously. In high school, I started taking Dexatrim and exercising compulsively. I thought cigarettes contributed to being able to control my weight, so I was afraid to quit smoking for fear of gaining weight. Also, I was very image conscious and aware of my body. I remember feeling like a slave to it.

The main thing that I feel contributed to my habit of smoking, initially, was rebellion. Doing exactly what my father didn't want me to do. At that point in my life, I thought freedom was being my own boss. That was something that my father hated. My parents despised smoking and never even had alcohol in the house. They were very strict, but also hypocritical because they did other things.

My parents discovered that I was smoking the summer when I was fifteen, and they forced me to eat a pack of cigarettes. Of course, I got sick and threw up. But, at that point I was mainly influenced by the crowd I was hanging around with. My girlfriends, and the boys we hung out with, all smoked because it was fun. I think it was one of those things they chose to ignore. Before school every morning I would sit outside in the backyard and have a cigarette before I got on the bus.

My current environment has a critical influence on my smoking behavior in general. I'm around people who believe that our body is a temple of God and I don't want to do anything to shorten my life or make myself unhealthy in any way. There is always a little seed of that in me, but I believe the pain of smoking is greater than resisting it. Also, I am not around smokers anymore, which makes a difference. I am a mortgage broker. No person in my office, family or church smokes.

I thought about quitting from the very first cigarette I smoked. It was always pretty gross and disgusting, but I became serious about quitting when I was pregnant. I did not smoke much during my pregnancy; I remember having only three cigarettes in nine months. My daughter, Maddy, is now six years old. Almost immediately after delivery, I started sneaking cigarettes again. I say sneaking because my husband didn't approve. I never smoked in the house, and mostly smoked on business trips after our daughter was born.

I started the Weigh Down Workshop (see reference in Appendix C). While I was losing weight from the program, I learned that we are all created with a hole in our heart and you can't take something away without replacing it, which is why I believe I've always gained weight every time I tried to quit smoking. I tried to quit many, many times before, but it never lasted. I learned in *Weigh Down*, that when I had an impulse to smoke or eat past the feeling of being full, to run to God instead.

In terms of my past occupations and current job, they absolutely affected my health behavior change. I was a regional sales manager for Bose, selling loud speakers for 10 years. From age 23, until I was 33, I was exposed to a rock-n-roll crowd. I traveled a lot. I would be on a plane Monday and come home on Thursday or Friday, having covered the Midwest. There were a lot of smokers, like myself, who were trying to quit but were away from home in hotel rooms and hotel bars. After a sales meeting that lasted about 10 hours, everyone would congregate at the bar for happy hour and cigarettes. I was making six figures and felt like I was a slave to my income. I was really miserable. I was smoking, drinking and hating my job. I felt as if I were missing my daughter's childhood. So I prayed about it and felt like I was awakening spiritually. I was listening to *Weigh Down* tapes, reading the Bible, and felt like my current situation was not what God wanted for me. I was completely controlled by money. I was a nut over the finances, but we were in debt. We had a lot of credit card debt and spent everything we made. The local supermarket called to congratulate us on being one of the top 1% of their customers because we would grocery shop everyday. We had a nanny that was taking care of our daughter and it just wasn't working, life wasn't working. So I started really praying and was inspired one night. I wrote a business plan for our family on how we were going to get out of debt. Within six months I was able to quit my six-figure job and stay at home with our daughter, which I did for two years. It was God and obedience. I feel like the pain of being enslaved by cigarettes, finances, or overeating was a miserable pit.

In terms of quitting, I tried everything; the patch, gum, switching cigarette brands, switching from menthol to non-menthol, only smoking half, or making the cigarettes so disgusting that I would be revolted. Nothing worked. Eventually it became a money issue. When I quit my job we went on a very strict budget. The nicotine gum was $40-$50 a week and I couldn't afford that anymore. I couldn't afford cigarettes either. I also didn't want my daughter to see me smoking. I just felt I got to a point where I wasn't able to do it on my own and that is when I learned how God can fill you up. Today, you couldn't pay me to smoke a cigarette or overeat. If I've eaten half of a candy bar and I'm full, you could not give me $1000 to eat that second half. You also couldn't pay me to over spend right now, and that used to be like a drug for me too. If I wasn't eating or smoking then I'd be shopping — the thrill from all of that is gone now.

I grew up going to a Lutheran church where all four of my grandparents were members. But the church seemed just inundated with sin, I don't know how else to say it. The pastor was sleeping with four-five women in the church. I left the church though high school, college and into my twenties.

When I had my daughter, Madeline, I was just completely overwhelmed by having a child that I loved beyond measure. I just felt like God was calling me back, so we joined a non-denominational church which seemed full of the Holy Spirit and we started to change a lot. I reduced the amount I was smoking, but was still "closet smoking". Our finances became more controlled and I began to make plans to quit my job. At the same time, my mother gave me tapes of the *Weigh Down Workshop* that she had been taking. I started to listen to them every morning, while I was obsessively exercising. I had to run five miles every morning and I was a slave to that too. One of the principles is that one shall have no other God than He. Before that, I never knew that a God could be in the form of food, a cigarette, wanting praise from my husband, or employer. Before my behavior change, I was depressed, overweight and weighed the most that I had ever weighed — about 180 pounds and was miserable.

My church, family, and others who were also making this change, were my support structure. Not being around those who would say, "Oh, it is OK that you overate, you can start again Monday" was helpful. It is important to surround yourself with people who feel you can do this. I am on the phone everyday with my girlfriend Jill, who has lost 80 pounds. Being around others that are making the same change is critical.

Regarding relapse, you overcome relapse by getting right back-up and running. Do not get bogged down with self analysis, or with beating yourself up over it.

I figured out there were certain times or occasions that I was more tempted than others. Being alone at night in front of the television was almost unbearable. Watching television or reading magazines while alone was a deadly combination, so I would just put on "armor" and plan ahead. When I'm tired, I go to bed. I don't watch television much, maybe 15 minutes, because that was a time when I was tempted to smoke or run to the store. I had to stay away from situations that were too tempting. I don't go to bars anymore. We just had work done on our basement, and the contractors smoked. When they were outside smoking, I didn't go and hang out with them. I ran the other way.

Regarding relapse, you overcome relapse by getting right back up and running. Do not get bogged down with self analysis, or with beating yourself up over it. "OK, so I smoked a cigarette — I'm not going to do it anymore." That used to be paralysis for me; I would become so depressed about smoking just one cigarette that I would want to smoke three more.

Every time I smoked a cigarette, and every time I took a cigarette out, I would resolve to quit. I hated it, but I was smoking 1 1/2 packs per day. When I was a sales rep I was working out of my home and it was easy to smoke, because I was alone. No one was there watching.

My life is so different now than it was three years ago. It was all about food, cigarettes and alcohol. My husband and I couldn't have dinner without a bottle of wine. Every night we would drink one or two bottles of wine, where now we sit out on the porch and maybe have one glass. But, it's not like we have to have it as we did before. Money is something we've also controlled. Food and money are things that you can't necessarily quit, like cigarettes. You still have to go shopping, you still have to eat. But I learned to eat naturally, within boundaries, which is very freeing.

Gwen S. was my role model for making this change. She wasn't a smoker, but she applied the principles to weight and she taught me how to replace my hunger for cigarettes with a hunger for God.

My motivation for change was that I wanted to clean my body and life. I wanted to not take my health for granted. I wanted to set a better example for my daughter and not be disgusting to my husband.

I didn't use the Internet, books or manuals to assist with my behavior change. I used the *Weigh Down* program principles. My physician was supportive of me quitting. He prescribed the nicotine patch and *Nicorette* gum, which was great because my insurance paid for it. The gum went over-the-counter, and was not covered by my insurance any longer, which was a good motivation to quit. I really enjoyed the gum. It was like getting a little kick that no one would know about — but with both, I still had nicotine in my system.

When I finally did quit smoking, I felt I was fully prepared to make the change. I don't think I will have trouble maintaining this change in the future. **If I had to do anything differently, I wouldn't have wasted so**

much time. My number one hope and prayer is that my daughter won't ever touch cigarettes. I will strongly encourage her to hang around kids that are living healthy natural lives, because smoking is unnatural.

I think I would say I am the "Reformer" personality. I hope that I'm characterized by self-control, purpose and principle. I do believe that you can go "all the way".

In summary, I believe that when I began these harmful behaviors I did it because I thought it represented freedom. I thought freedom was doing whatever I wanted to do, but now I believe that freedom is doing what God wants me to do. I believe God wants me to be healthy. He wants me to take care of my body. He wants me to have loving, supporting relationships, not angry relationships. God wants health in every sense. Freedom is in obedience, in obeying God, which is the exact opposite of what I thought it was growing up. The advice I have for others is don't give up. Don't give up, don't give up, don't give up — and run to God. That's what finally did it for me. I had tried everything and finally I just got to the end of myself.

Randy C.

53-Year-Old Male
Flint, MI
Quit Smoking

I am 53 years-old, married and male with four children. I was raised lower class, in Flint, Michigan with my five siblings. I attended some college and am now a middle class factory worker.

The health behavior change I successfully implemented was quitting smoking. I just stopped smoking "cold turkey" and didn't use anything to assist me. I made this change five months ago. I made two previous attempts to quit smoking. During the course of making this change I did feel like I wanted to start smoking again, but I just told myself "no." My original motivation to make this change was when I awoke one morning with a terrible cough and the taste of smoke in my mouth.

My wife provided me with the most support however, I relied mostly on myself to make this change. My entire family — brothers, sisters, kids and friends also gave me support. I didn't use written materials, the Internet, or professional help to assist me in quitting. I don't know if my physician knows about my behavior change. My role model was my uncle as he hasn't smoked for 10 years. My uncle smoked his entire life, but within the last 10 years he has not had one cigarette. No relapse at all.

My recommendation for others is you have to want to change. No one can make the change for you. My personality type is the "Achiever". I could see the finish line and tasted the success. I set out a goal and tackled it head-on. I felt very prepared to quit smoking.

The timing was right. I felt there was no time like the present. I had to stop and it was just a matter of time. That morning was the right day and time. If I could do anything differently I wouldn't have developed another bad habit, in addition to smoking. I was also drinking. One thing that was crucial to my success was not hanging around the negative influences. I am not on the scene like I used to be — not at local bars or hangout spots.

Shirlee B.

53-Year-Old Female
Ohio
Increased Physical Activity
Weight Loss
Diabetes Management

I am 53 years-old married and female, with one child. I am a college graduate. I was one of five siblings, raised in a lower-middle class family. I spent most of my childhood in Ohio. I am an administrative assistant. I consider myself, currently, to be middle class.

The behavior changes I made were increasing my physical activity to two times per week for eight months, losing weight and keeping my diabetes under control.

For me, a successful change is making the right food choices and having good eating habits.

I made this behavior change eight months ago. I had previously made four other attempts to make these changes in my life. The original motivation for making the change was that I was tired of being overweight. I also have a daughter that I want to see grow into a beautiful woman.

My family, friends and co-workers supported me. I mostly relied on my husband. He never pushed me, but just supported my decisions. I also received support from co-workers. They would say nice comments to me, and that helped. **I am doing this change with a close friend.** I didn't use written materials or media to assist with my changes. I didn't use the Internet either, but I did seek professional help by joining *Weight Watchers.*

My physician knows about my behavior changes, and is very supportive and helpful. My doctor encouraged me to continue and said that it was possible. I also have a role model.

I don't think I will have trouble maintaining this change in the future. My sister is a diabetic and did the same things I am doing, with wonderful results.

A recommendation I would give to others is to use *Weight Watchers*. Think of this as healthy living, not a diet.

The personality type that best matches me is the "Individualist".

I wanted to have personal goals. I wanted to do this health behavior change on my own, without a doctor telling me I had to. My source of motivation was reaching my goal. I felt like I was very prepared for this change. The timing was right when I started. I said to myself, "Just because my feet are constantly hurting and I can't feel my toes, I am not about to let this beat me." At the same time, my friend was ready to make a similar change also, which helped.

If I were to do it again, I wouldn't do anything differently. Self-esteem was crucial to my success. It was down, but I need to pull it back up for myself and for my family.

Beryl H.

66-Year-Old Female

Tacoma, WA

Diabetes Management

My name is Berly H. I am 66 years-old and female. I am a college graduate, and currently retired. I am married with three children. I grew up in Tacoma, Washington with two siblings, in a middle class home, and now consider myself to be middle class.

My health behavior change that I accomplished is walking at least two miles a day, in addition to exercising three times per week. I incorporated exercise with healthier eating and turned my life around. As a result, I am able to keep my diabetes under control.

Another successful change I accomplished three years ago is looking and feeling better. Previously, I had never attempted this behavior. My first motivation to make this change was due to complications at my annual physical. My daughter, who is a Registered Nurse, was my support in making these changes but I mostly relied on my husband. He does everything with me. Family and friends all helped in different ways as well. I used written materials and professional help to assist me with this change. My physician was also supportive. She directed me on the right path and was determined to make me healthier. In making these changes, I didn't have a role model. I don't know of anyone who accomplished these behavior changes before me however, I do know people who are attempting these changes now. I give them support, advice and prayer. I don't think I will have trouble maintaining exercise and eating healthier in the future.

I would recommend that others take one day at a time, and plan exercise activities and healthy meals in advance. Don't focus on the

negatives. For example, don't look at what you can't eat, look at all you can eat for many years to come.

My personality type is the "Helper". I took my disease of diabetes and turned it into an example. I show others that it can be done. I can beat this and overcome it. I look and feel much better. I enjoy life and all that it has to offer.

I did not feel very prepared for this change at all. Other forces caused me to make this change. My doctor informed me that I had diabetes and I was admitted to the hospital. I then took insulin for three weeks. I had no choice but to change my behavior so I could live a healthier life and eventually stop taking insulin. **(Caution — See statement at the end of this story)** Regarding my health behavior changes — I wouldn't do anything differently, because I faced it head-on.

One thing that is crucial to my success is lots of prayer. The "All-mighty" is my reason for everything. God got me through it.

Caution: In an effort to allow each interviewee to tell his or her own story, all statements made were left unchanged. Most diabetics that begin taking insulin must take it for the rest of their lives. It is recommended that the prescribing physician be consulted before changing or discontinuing the use of any prescribed medication.

Becky M. (sic)

24-Year-Old Female
Mead, NE
Weight Loss

My name is Becky M. I am 24 years-old married and female with no children. I am a college graduate with two brothers, and I grew up in Mead, Nebraska. I currently work as a secretary.

I have lost about 108 pounds. I have a little bit more to lose to be healthy for my age and height. This behavior change has been a total turnaround for me. I have been overweight my whole life. Both my parents are overweight. I used to not even think about what I was eating and just ate whatever was around. As I became older, I ate more and didn't worry about the food being healthy. I don't know if it is genetic — I think it is more environmental.

Slowly, I changed what I was eating and started to exercise. I had been on yo-yo diets since high school — probably for eight or nine years. I feel like I went through stages. **When I first started changing my eating habits, I just focused on portion sizes. I wasn't necessarily eating the right food, but eating less of it. After a few months, I also began to change <u>what</u> I was eating.** I started eating whole grains and more fruits and vegetables. **Then, after another couple of months, I physically began to move more. Prior to this point in time, I was really inactive. I started to walk more. At work, the grocery store, or mall I would park further from the entrance.** I did that for a few months and then started to exercise at the wellness center regularly, which I am still doing. I am in a phase where exercise is important to me, and I really make an effort to do it. I go to the wellness center nearly every day now.

The people, both at work and outside of work, who provided me with the support I needed to make this health behavior change were my husband, family, parents and friends. Also the people at the wellness center provided support. I mainly rely on my husband and friends at work.

When I first started changing my eating habits, I just focused on portion sizes. I wasn't necessarily eating the right food, but eating less of it. After a few months, I also began to change what I was eating.

Some women at work had made changes in their exercise and eating habits before me, and they helped me get started. My husband is trying his best to make changes, and is very supportive when deciding what food we bring into the house. Half of the success is not having the "wrong food" around. The people at work are great. They used to have food days, and the food would be right by my desk. It's not there anymore. Now I bring something healthy, and others do too. That's really helpful. You don't feel like you are depriving yourself of anything.

My husband is also helpful when I try new recipes. Sometimes when cooking "low-fat" it can also be "low taste" but he has always been a good sport, trying everything. My husband also goes to the store and makes a big effort to buy food that won't be tempting to me. If he is in the mood for sweets, he will just buy a single serving or one candy bar, and not a gallon of ice cream. He is also supportive of my exercising. I want to run the *Corporate Cup* (see reference in Appendix C) this Fall so I am starting to train for it.

My parents have been great. My older brother was in *Weight Watchers* a couple years ago, and was successful. He has been supportive and cheers me on.

I used *Weight Watchers* (see reference in Appendix C) books, point finders, and cook books. I used the Internet a lot to find recipes. I just searched, *Weight Watchers* and thousands of sites came up with meal points. This makes calculating your points very easy. I also really relied on the expertise of the *Weight Watchers* leaders.

My physician does know about my change. I hadn't been in for a while, and when I returned I had lost approximately 50 pounds. He was so surprised. He is really supportive and a big fan of the *Weight Watchers* program. My physician is really happy I am not on a "fad" diet.

I don't think I will have trouble maintaining this health behavior change because it is now engrained in me. **Really, it's not a diet for me anymore, it's the way I am and the way I live my life now.** I really don't think about going back to my past weight because it is so far from who I am now.

My motivation to change was a couple things: **I had two friends at work making changes and I just started thinking, "Other people are doing it — maybe I can too."** I especially remember the week before the first meeting (*Weight Watchers*). I had the idea of losing weight in my mind forever. Then I spent a couple of months thinking about joining *Weight Watchers*. Then I was to the point where I thought, "If I die tomorrow, I will die fat and unhappy with the way I have treated myself." I look back and realize that there were days I was unhappy with the way I treated my body. I now feel my body is a gift and I should be grateful for it. I treated it poorly for so long — I felt I could not continue the way it was. Even though change would be hard, it would be easier than living the way I had been.

The new thinking was a "light bulb moment". When I started the health behavior change I was 23 years old, and my knees hurt. I remember thinking, "I am young and this is just wrong." I shouldn't have pain walking up stairs. My role model was a girl at work who did really great and lost a lot of weight on *Weight Watchers*. When I joined, there was a lady who lost 100 pounds. For a while, I thought, "I have so much to lose, I will never get to my goal weight," but there was someone who proved it could be done.

Regarding recommendations for others, I would say the biggest thing would be to make changes you can live with for the rest of your life. **I tried so many "fad" diets and they worked for a while, but it was just impossible to live with them permanently.** It has to be something you are comfortable with. Also, do not expect everything to change overnight. **I made slow and small changes here and there — and it all added up to where my lifestyle is completely different now. It's not a diet, it's a *lifestyle*.** In the beginning, when I passed on a dessert, people would ask, "Are you on a diet?" I would reply, "Yes." But now I don't answer that way because it is my lifestyle. It is just how I behave. It's the choices I make and I choose to make different choices than in my past.

Charles D.

35-Year-Old Male

St. Louis, MO

Weight Loss

My name is Charles D. I was born in St. Louis, Missouri and still live here now. I am 35 years-old, divorced and a high school graduate.

I was always very active as a kid. I played sports all through high school. I was captain of the football team, and very fit. Then I got married when I was a senior in high school. After that, I had to shift priorities. Instead of working out I had to provide for my family. I started working. Then over the years just working, traveling with work, and raising a family, I got out of the exercise mode. Over the course of 10 years or so, I put on some weight.

I have two brothers and two sisters. I am the youngest of the bunch. Growing up our health behaviors were good, very healthy. We were always active, always outside playing, or doing an organized sport for physical activity. We had track meets up the road. All of us would go and do events. We would get ribbons for it. As a kid, I remember both of my parents being very active in the track meets.

Over the years, as I was putting on weight, I would just buy the next larger pant size, so I would feel comfortable. On occasion, I would lose 5 to10 pounds and then put it back on, due to being inactive or eating a lot. Because I traveled quite a bit, and was on the go all the time, it was hard. What really hit me was when my father had a stroke in July of 1999. He was 68, and had barely been retired for three years. That was the first time there was a family health issue. About a year later I had my cholesterol checked and it was sky high. They wanted me to go on medication, but I said, "No, I can control it on my own." After that I would exercise a little by bike riding and walking, but that was it. The fact that I needed to change didn't really have a full-impact on me until my mother died of a massive heart attack $1^1/2$ years later.

My sister Katie, my next sibling up, was concerned about me. My sister has always been in such good physical shape. She was a swimmer and graduated from St. Louis University School of Public Health. She is a dietician. She said, "Let's get you going." At the time, my response was "No." I was resistant. One day she got a postcard from The American Stroke Association (see reference in Appendix C). It said, "Training for a marathon is a life-changing event like having a stroke, come find out about this program." She looked into it and asked if I wanted to do it.

I had always wanted to run a marathon, but never thought I could. In 1986, I bought a book on running and training for a marathon and it sat on my bookshelf for all those years. I just never really felt like I could do it. In November of 2001, my sister and I went to the meeting put on by The American Stroke Association. It was about training for a marathon in Hawaii. You had to raise a specific amount of money and fund your way. Both my sister and I looked at each other and said, "Hey, we need a good thing." We signed up there on the spot and completed the marathon in 2002!

In November of 2001 I weighed 258 pounds. We signed up and started fundraising in December. I talked to a lot of people about what I was doing, but I never really put it into action. Then I realized that I would have to train for this. I couldn't just talk about it. In late December, I started walking. I could barely walk half of a mile without becoming winded. Then we started getting into it. In mid January I joined a gym and, from that point on, I was a regular on the fast track.

The marathon was in six months. I dropped 65 pounds in $4^1/2$ months. I went from 250 to185 pounds. I started out slow. I didn't need to go on a diet. A lot of people go up and down. They take the weight off, then put it right back on. **What I did, was instead of eating a whole pizza, I would eat half. I would just eat in moderation and watch portions. Also I was exercising.**

I was exercising by myself or with my sister once a week but, I needed more support. So I asked a friend, whom I knew was a cyclist and not a runner, if she would run with me. She said, "I don't run, but I'll bike and do other activities." So we ended up doing things together. We did everything; bike riding, walking, running, and in-line skating. I would awaken in the morning and use the elliptical trainer. I started out with 15 minutes the first time, then built-up to the point where, in about a month, I was doing 60 minutes. Then, with friends, I would usually get in a second workout in the evening by biking, in-line skating or running. Occasionally I would take one day off. My friend was an inspiration to me. I knew when I was slacking; I needed to reach out to certain people and say, "Here's what I am doing, I need help."

Getting started was the most difficult. Everyone wants to lose weight without any effort by taking a pill. There were a couple months where I was really struggling to change my habits. I was going from being non-active to being active. During that initial stage is when I reached out to other people. One was my sister. Since we could not work out together, we would ask one another on the phone, "What exercise did you do today? How was your workout?" We would keep in touch that way. I had a couple people really cheering me on and keeping me going during that first hump.

That initial stage, from mid December 2001 until mid February 2002, was tough. Then I got into it, I really got into it! It came down to when I missed a day, I really felt bad. On my days off, I felt like I should be doing something. Once I began, it took about two months to arrive at that point. I eventually would wake at 5:00 AM and go to the gym for an hour, then go to work an hour early. I felt like I had more energy. I used to drink a lot of soda and I replaced that with water. Right now, I don't drink any soda! During my initial stage, I gave up coffee as well. I now have a couple cups in the morning.

What I did, was instead of eating a whole pizza, I would eat half. I would just eat in moderation and watch portions. Also I was exercising.

When you are eating on the road, you have a wide-range of options available. You don't always pick foods that are the best for you. I had a good expense account so I could eat whatever I wanted — and I did!

Another thing is your mindset. A lot of people, and I know I have done it, think when they get up in the morning that they are going to workout in the afternoon. But, by the time the afternoon comes they don't have time for exercise. That is why I discovered working out first thing in the morning is a key. Everyone says, "Well, I don't have time." There are no excuses. I used to do the same thing, but really, everyone has an hour if they just wake up an hour earlier.

When I am on the road, the first thing I do is work out. Usually, the places I stay at have a mini gym. If they don't, I will get up and run a couple miles. The American Stroke Association has some tips, and one of them is to get the right equipment for training. For example, don't just go out and buy a pair of running shoes, go out and get fitted and buy the right shoe. I found that was something very important. Actually, I did that, made the investment and got the right gear. I just remember one thing they said, "Cotton is rotten, and you know it when you are working out." There is a dry fit fabric that pulls the moisture away from your body. So, I got the right type of clothes to exercise in. That was a change I made.

I just had to make that investment and it really paid off.

Being fit and making a lifetime change is something that you just can't do for six months and then go back to your old habits. It is something that you have to be conscience of every day. Let's say you overeat and it is a constant struggle every day not to. Then it is important to have support with others so you can talk about it. I kept a training diary of my workouts and that helped. I can go back and look at it everyday. I can look at the weeks when I didn't do anything and realize, "Oh my gosh! I gained five pounds." Well, yeah, it's because I haven't been doing anything.

In the past, I tried to lose weight at least once every-other year. The year before, if someone would have said that I was going to lose 65 pounds and be in the best shape of my life, I would have said, "No way." I used to have the hardest time just losing five pounds. Weight is something that I struggled with for many years. My initial goal was not to lose 65 pounds, but to lose 30. I surpassed that and kept bringing it down and down.

Before I began exercising, I went to my doctor for high cholesterol and was placed on *Lipitor*. This is an issue I have a family history of. My father had high cholesterol and so do I. I was on *Lipitor* for a couple months, but after I started losing weight, I stopped taking it. **(Caution — See statement at the end of this story)** My doctor said, "The medicine is working." And I said, "No, actually, I haven't taken it for two months." So, I brought down my cholesterol levels by watching what I ate and the quantity, and then just adding exercise.

Once you start working out, you look at people like Lance Armstrong, and they inspire you. Last year, I did my first triathlon. Since then, I have been training for a number of different ones. This past year, I did my first half Ironman. I finished in five hours and 47 minutes. My goal is to do a full Ironman next fall.

My doctor was not helpful. When I was at 250 pounds, he would say, "Oh, you are a couple of pounds overweight," like I only needed to lose a couple of pounds and it wasn't really a big deal. I am a believer in finding out as much as you can about sports and training on your own. The American Stroke Association gave me resources I felt were very helpful. Since then, I have purchased several books on topics like running a marathon and stretching. I have a number of different books on triathlons and have a "training bible".

Now I am to the point where I need to have a coach to help me get through the full Ironman. There are certain things that you can do by yourself, but then you need help from other skilled people. That is something I would like to encourage for everyone: To make a lifestyle change, find a partner that has the same goal. Having someone who is depending on you to be there will help motivate both of you.

Caution: In an effort to allow each interviewee to tell his or her own story, all statements made were left unchanged. It is recommended that the prescribing physician be consulted before changing or discontinuing the use of any prescribed medication.

Don D.

51-Year-Old Male
Kalamazoo, MI/Indianapolis, IN
Weight Loss

I was born in Kalamazoo, Michigan and am now living in Indianapolis, Indiana. I am 51 years-old, male, married, and have a Ph.D. in entomology — the study of bugs. I have a fairly uneventful, normal life. I grew up in a family of six. There were four children in my family — I am the second child. My mother and father both worked "blue-collar" jobs.

I was diagnosed with Type II diabetes about three years ago. In one sense, being diagnosed was not a big surprise because it was weight-related. I am a big guy, at 6'5", so I carry my weight without looking obese. I had always been a big kid, and as an adult, a big guy. But, I have never been "Subway Jared" obese. I had always been a few pounds over my ideal weight, but it was never important enough to motivate me to do something about it. It's that simple. I was diagnosed during a routine cholesterol screening with my family doctor. My physician shared, "Your sugar numbers are so high that I can't get an accurate cholesterol reading." I took this as a big surprise because in the past, this was never an issue during my annual screenings for cholesterol and glucose. Then, boom! All of a sudden, just like that, my blood glucose numbers were very high.

I have a family history of Type II diabetes. My grandmother was diagnosed with Type II diabetes, but she was in her seventies. My father was also in his seventies when he was diagnosed. Being 47 years old, I was a bit surprised. I began addressing it immediately. Interestingly, my family physician is also my next-door neighbor. We were out for a walk on a Sunday afternoon. She stopped me and said, "You have diabetes." In disbelief, I said, "What?" A couple of days later I had an appointment with her, and she showed me the numbers. I thought it was a fluke — a mistake. I went home and pricked my finger. The average should have been 100 or less, and I was over 300. I thought the machine was not working, so I gave it to my wife who tried it on herself and she got an 86. I then knew it wasn't the machine. My doctor said the diabetes was obviously weight related. She shared that some patients are able to watch their diet, exercise, and weight, and keep their diabetes under control. She said, "Before I put you on any medication, I would like you to try making these changes." This was fine with me because I really didn't want to be on medication. So that is where I began. Immediately, I went to diabetes and nutrition classes, which my doctor recommended. I attended one for about an hour and said, "This is silly, and I know all of this stuff." I had enough biochemistry and nutrition in college, and therefore knew what I was supposed to do; it was just a matter of doing it at that point. My lifestyle was not very healthy however, I had been exercising three times a week prior to my diagnosis. At work we have an outstanding health facility where I have been going for a couple years, three times a week. What I hadn't done was control my diet. I had pretty unhealthy eating habits. I would skip breakfast or lunch, then go home at night and binge. By not eating breakfast or lunch, my metabolism was basically shutting down.

Now, I have three meals a day. I eat a small breakfast and lunch, and then much more moderate dinners; absolutely no snacks. I used to be known as the "Donut King" around work. If there were donuts anywhere, I would find them. I now know moderation is key. You can eat pretty much anything you want as long as you don't eat very much of it, especially if you can avoid the simple sugars. Starches aren't so bad if you don't eat too many of them. Like I said, this is knowledge that I had, it was just that I wasn't practicing what I knew. I don't think any part of my poor health was work-related. If anything, my company does an outstanding job of promoting health. They sponsor full-blown employee health screenings every other year. It's really just a matter of people taking advantage of these services. We have a great workout facility here onsite with an outstanding staff and trainers. Two trainers in particular were very helpful to me. One was specialized in cardiovascular fitness, and the other with free weights. When I first started exercising daily, I dropped weight and felt really good about how I was starting to look. I started reading health and fitness magazines. It made me realize that losing weight was not enough, so I started working out with free weights. I was amazed how I started to look and feel with the combination of losing weight and body building. I was looking better than when I was in my twenties. Both of those trainers in the fitness center were very helpful, encouraging, and taught me a lot. They were very supportive.

For me, I found the blood glucose strips to be a very positive reinforcement. Very early on, I was able to track my baseline sugar readings. It was a very immediate, positive reinforcement for me. I still test once a day every morning, I just don't do it four-five times a day like I used to. I have my blood glucose tested enough now that my doctor is very comfortable with where I am. What is interesting about being diagnosed with diabetes is that I never had symptoms, which is why it came as such a shock for me. They say it is a silent disease. Your blood sugar could be high for a long time but you would never know it. It is when your blood sugar goes way down that you start to get lightheaded symptoms, which was never an issue for me. I was at a point where I had to get up several times during the night and urinate. At the time, I just thought, "I am getting older and that is what happens to old guys." Now I realize what it really was.

During the last six months, I am not sure if you could call it a relapse, but I'm not as disciplined on my diet as I used to be. I've noticed that I've gained a little weight. I am certainly not where I was. Consequently, there is an immediate increase in my baseline sugar level correlating with my weight. The last month I started to watch myself more carefully again and, sure enough, my baseline went back down. In my case, diabetes is control-

label, I think this is because I caught it early enough. I thank my doctor for that. I was exercising, but not enough. My friend at work and I exercise a lot together. **I don't think it is possible to exercise enough to outweigh the amount of food you eat. Exercise by itself without regulating intake of food will not allow you to lose weight.** My friend and I work out regularly, five to seven days a week. We do high-powered workouts, 600-700 calories a session. The moment I started to increase my snacks and portion sizes, the weight started to come back. If you don't watch your intake at this age, all the exercise in the world is not going to help.

I had the knowledge, it was just the discipline I lacked. It was the wake up call of diabetes that said, "Look, you have got to fix what you are doing."

Regarding environmental changes, I am not sure if it is that or just avoiding temptations. There is always food available at work. It is just a matter of making the decision to not eat that donut, cake or whatever. We are doing some behavioral work in one of my projects at work. **One of the results we found is that consequences really modify behavior. If the consequence is certain and immediate, there is a greater chance that a behavior change will occur.** Just knowing that I was testing my blood glucose level every morning of every day, was an immediate consequence as well as an absolute certainty.

We bought a treadmill and weight bench for our home. My wife works out too, and we purchased the treadmill primarily for her. Eventually I started to use it.

Vacations are my biggest barriers, because they remove me from my environment and out of my workout routine. A couple years ago we took a two-week vacation to China. It was interesting to go jogging in China. We received many looks from the locals. I exercised, but not every day. I couldn't do my weight lifting, so when I returned it was very hard to get back to my weight lifting routine. Work is actually the best time for me to exercise. It is almost the highlight of my workday, so I can forget about things for an hour. I find weekends challenging to stay on my exercise routine. I have bad knees, and that is probably the biggest barrier. Even walking fast is difficult on my knees. What's nice about the health center at work is we have elliptical machines with zero percent impact. You get a great workout. So when I am away from the office, it is hard for me to exercise because I find it too painful.

I didn't have a role model. My wife is pretty fit and has been seeing a personal trainer for years. She is someone who can eat chocolate or chips and not gain weight — so she is not much of a role model in that way. I paged through the book Body for Life (see reference in Appendix C), and that was somewhat motivational — seeing the before and after pictures.

I never did have to take diabetes medication. I felt totally prepared for making my health behavior change — the issue was actually just having the motivation to do it. The message of excess weight and the risk for diabetes is there, but it seems like nobody listens. We lived in Europe for about four years, and the stereotype is that the typical American is 20-50 pounds overweight. When we moved back, we noticed how true this stereotype seemed. Its sad how many people are overweight. If one could see into their future and the consequences of their health behavior, people may behave differently. Again, it is that consequence that is uncertain and in the future, so the behavior doesn't change.

Managing my diabetes in the future is a concern, because I work out hard at 51 years old. I think I can do this for another 10-15 years, but at some point in my life I may not be able to anymore. Exercise alone is not enough. I think if I can maintain how much I eat, then I will be OK — it is just knowing my glucose levels — as long as I have my glucose monitor. That is my long-term strategy.

Regarding the personality assessment: I can pick out pieces of almost half of them that fit me, but I don't see one that is just totally me. I went over the personality types several times. I am mostly the "Enthusiast" and the "Individualist".

Frank and Juanita E.

60-Year-Old Male and 58-Year-Old Female
Toledo, OH/Gaithesburg, SC
Quit Smoking

My name is Frank E. I was born in Toledo, Ohio in 1942. I'm 60 years-old and married. I completed high school and an apprenticeship in machinery repair.

My name is Juanita E. I've always gone by the name of "Nita" and never my full name. I was born in Toledo, Ohio in 1944. I am a 58 years-old, female and married to Frank. I received my Master's degree in education. We now live on a lake in Gaithesburg, South Carolina.

(Nita): We had a significant change in our smoking habits. Beyond smoking we have also made significant changes in our overall lifestyle.

(Frank): It all evolved from quitting smoking.

(Nita): As a teacher, I had always been somewhat active, but I did have some bad habits; including smoking and drinking alcohol. I have always been active — walking, ice skating, doing water sports — but I was not ever involved in any endurance activities.

(Frank): **I smoked for years because it was the norm — I was a factory worker, and smoking and drinking was accepted behavior in that environment.**

(Nita): I attended a volleyball match for teachers 22 years ago, and a friend said to me, "Lets run one mile on the track," but I was afraid to do it. My friend pushed me to join her, and she did the run slow enough to allow me to be able to finish it. That was critical because I was afraid, and being a smoker, running was not the easiest thing. It was not completely outside of my capability though because I had always been somewhat active. Later, under the cover of night, I went back and ran two miles. I did this at night several more times at my own comfortable pace so that I would not feel too self conscious about it. Over a little time I got up to four miles.

There were some influential teachers in the school system that developed into a support group. That made a big difference because our activities were fun. The more I ran the more I started to view food as fuel and not as something purely for pleasure. That is when my smoking decreased, and eventually stopped, and healthier activities increased.

About this time, a former student invited me to come in to his Nautilus (see reference in Appendix C) center and attend some sessions. This was important for me because I had been trained not to hurt myself. I was never allowed to cut the grass at my house when I was younger or allowed to exert myself physically, but the guy at Nautilus pushed me a little bit. I worked out on my own once I was trained in how to use the system, and I did this with my daughter. I was able to learn at my own comfortable pace, and then I came back harder. This was important for me because, with the development of mental toughness, I was able to increase my levels of exercise.

(Frank): **Now we work out because it's a social thing. We really look forward to working out with our friends.** We work out a lot; we run 2 days a week with a running group, and we are the oldest people in the group. We do speed work at the track, and we enjoy the company of others. Recently, my team placed in a Marine Corps fitness run/obstacle course. I am very competitive. But mostly, I choose to exercise because it's a fun and social thing.

(Nita): When we were running a lot, it would be inconvenient when we went to my mom's house. At breakfast time we would choose to go out and run and when we would come back after the workout, the kitchen would be closed. At first my mom thought that I was nuts, but when she got sick and was getting ready to pass on, she told me not to stop running. **My mother recognized the fact that because Frank and I were exercising, we were able to maintain functionality.**

(Nita): I am very active in my church, and even with all of the other things going on in my life, I choose to make the time for exercise. It's important to me that I have time to exercise. I do not want to give that up, even when there are forces pulling against me.

(Frank): We were ready to change and began with the appropriate level and intensity of exercise. **It helped a lot to have the support of a group that made exercise social and fun. That has allowed us to maintain a high level of fitness and functionality as we move into our 60's.**

Since beginning our exercise program, we have done some things we never dreamed were possible. Nita did the Hawaiian Ironman in 1986 (I was a spectator.) In 1987 we both did it on the day of our 25th wedding anniversary. In 1988 we both ran in the Boston Marathon. In March of 2000 we attempted an adventure race in North Carolina, but we dropped out after 22 hours and 43 minutes for missing a check point deadline. Only 5 teams out of 60 finished the whole race, but that's another story.

Nita has returned to triathlons; having done an Olympic distance event last September, she is presently training for two more this year. I haven't been re-bitten by the triathlon bug yet, but I am really getting into mountain biking. We did a 10 day Great Divide mountain bike tour last year in Colorado. It was a guided, but self contained, trip of about 250 miles. It was hard work and a lot of fun.

We have both suffered some injuries this past year, but we are finally back up to full training schedules. The old bodies don't heal as fast as they used to.

Nita and I were recently talking about this — we've lived together a long time. We have been with each other longer than we were with our parents as children. We started out young, dating in high school. As a youngster, my parents smoked all the time. They socialized and partied with friends — that is what they did in that era. They would have card parties, music parties, etc.

> It helped a lot to have the support of a group that made exercise social and fun. That has allowed us to maintain a high level of fitness and functionality as we move into our 60's.

People would come over and drink and smoke all the time. That was accepted behavior. When I was a youngster, the only thing I heard was if you smoked it will stunt your growth. Nobody ever talked about cancer, heart attacks or other health conditions. **Smoking and drinking was an accepted lifestyle I was raised around and consequently, I started smoking at a young age.** I would sneak out and smoke "corn silk". I don't think kids even know how to do that anymore — they just start right out with cigarettes.

By the time I was 16, I would say, I was a smoker — and hooked. I guess I didn't think it was good for me, but I didn't think it was horrible for me either, until later on. Consequently, we smoked for quite a number of years. I don't think Nita even smoked until she met me.

(Nita): I started smoking shortly after I had our son, Tim, when I was 21.

(Frank): Then, even as a young family, that lifestyle carried over from what we learned from our parents and their friends. Smoking was evolutionary. It just evolved from watching our parents. **Our behavior even influenced our children and they eventually ended up smoking.** They were probably in high school when they started smoking.

Together, in 1983, we quit smoking. We now live very healthy and active lifestyles. I guess some would say more healthy and active than most people!

Appendices

Appendix A — Participant Story Interview Guide

The following list contains the questions used to guide each interview:

1. To start please state your full name, where you were born and live now, age, gender, marital status and education level.

2. Let's talk about your upbringing going back as far as you would like and then bring us up-to-date. Feel free to go back as far as required to help explain how you originally began the behavior you later changed, and the impact of your upbringing on the change process.

3. Follow up questions to explore when the interviewee started thinking about changing/controlling the behavior. If major sections of their life were left out, ask briefly why if it is potentially pertinent. Research anything you think might be helpful related to the behavior change. Ask if there was a family history/habit for the behavior being discussed.

4. How have the households you grew up in, your life path, and your current environment influenced your health in general and the behavior in question?

5. How has your past occupation(s) and current job affected your health and behavior change?

6. Describe what it was like when you first discovered you wanted to change or get this behavior under control. Do you think you have gone through stages since that initial decision or event? If yes describe.

7. Describe how you went about making the behavior change. Identify steps or milestones you took and accomplished along the way.

8. What support/support structure did you have while making the change (family, friends co-workers, etc.)?

9. How important was it to make environmental changes — changes in home, car, work, etc. or changes in where they went for recreation or to eat?

10. What barriers did you face during your successful attempt? Did you relapse? How did you overcome relapse?

11. How many times did you attempt to change the behavior before you were successful?

12. What other health behaviors have you successfully changed?

13. Did you have a role model for this successful change?

14. What was your motivation for making the change?

15. What did you use to help make the change (Internet, book(s) manuals, counseling, coaching, help from a health professional, etc.)? If a person helped you, who was it? Did your physician help? If yes how?

16. Did you use any medication(s)? If yes, were they OTC, prescription or both?

17. How prepared did you feel for making the change?

18. What would you do differently if having to do it again?

19. Do you think you will have trouble maintaining the change in the future?

20. Describe your personality type and how you feel it helped or hindered your success. Choose **one** option that best describes you (based on the Enneagram Institute's Riso-Hudson Enneagram Type Indicator*):

*For information regarding the Enneagram personality inventory visit: www.enneagraminstitute.com

_____ **The Reformer** (Conscientious with strong personal convictions: has an intense sense of right and wrong, personal religious and moral values. Dissatisfied with reality, they become high-minded idealists, feeling that it is up to them to improve everything. Can be highly dogmatic, self-righteous, intolerant, and inflexible. Want to be right, to strive higher and improve everything, to be consistent with their ideals, to justify themselves, to be beyond criticism so as not to be condemned by anyone.)

_____ **The Helper** (Empathetic, compassionate, feeling for others. Caring and concerned about their needs. Want to be closer to others, so start "people pleasing", becoming overly friendly, emotionally demonstrative, and full of "good intentions" about everything. Can be manipulative and self-serving, instilling guilt by telling others how much they owe them and make them suffer. Want to be loved, to express their feelings for others, to be needed and appreciated, to get others to respond to them, to vindicate their claims about themselves.)

_____ **The Achiever** (Self-assured, energetic, and competent with high self-esteem: they believe in themselves and their own value. Highly concerned with their performance, doing their job well, constantly driving self to achieve goals as if self-worth depends on it. Fearing failure and humiliation, they can be exploitative and opportunistic, covetous of the success of others, and willing to do "whatever it takes" to preserve the illusion of their superiority. Want to be affirmed, to distinguish themselves from others, to have attention, to be admired, and to impress others.)

_____ **The Individualist** (Self-aware, introspective, on the "search for self," aware of feelings and inner impulses. Take an artistic, romantic orientation to life, creating a beautiful, aesthetic environment to cultivate and prolong personal feelings. When dreams fail, become self-inhibiting and angry at self, depressed and alienated from self and others, blocked and emotionally paralyzed. Want to express themselves and their individuality, to create and surround themselves with beauty, to maintain certain moods and feelings, to withdraw to protect their self-image, to take care of emotional needs before attending to anything else, to attract a "rescuer".)

_____ **The Investigator** (Observe everything with extraordinary perceptiveness and insight. Begin conceptualizing and fine-tuning everything before acting — working things out in their minds: model building, preparing, practicing, and gathering more resources. Become reclusive and isolated from reality, eccentric and nihilistic. Want to possess knowledge, to understand the environment, to have everything figured out as a way of defending the self from threats from the environment.)

_____ **The Loyalist** (Able to elicit strong emotional responses from others: very appealing, endearing, lovable, affectionate. Start investing their time and energy into whatever they believe will be safe and stable. Fearing that they have ruined their security, they become panicky, volatile, and self-disparaging with acute inferiority feelings. Want to have security, to feel supported by others, to have certitude and reassurance, to test the attitudes of others toward them, to fight against anxiety and insecurity.)

_____ **The Enthusiast** (Highly responsive, excitable, enthusiastic about sensation and experience. As restlessness increases, want to have more options and choices available to them. Desperate to quell their anxieties, can be impulsive and infantile: do not know when to stop. Want to maintain their freedom and happiness, to avoid missing out on worthwhile experiences, to keep themselves excited and occupied, to avoid and discharge pain.)

_____ **The Challenger** (Self-assertive, self-confident, and strong: have learned to stand up for what they need and want. Self-sufficiency, financial independence, and having enough resources are important concerns: become enterprising, pragmatic, "rugged individualists," wheeler-dealers. Defying any attempt to control them, become completely ruthless, dictatorial, "might makes right." Want to be self-reliant, to prove their strength and resist weakness, to be important in their world, to dominate the environment, and to stay in control of their situation.)

_____ **The Peacemaker** (Deeply receptive, accepting, unselfconscious, emotionally stable and serene. Fear conflicts, so become self-effacing and accommodating, idealizing others and "going along" with their wishes, saying "yes" to things they do not really want to do. Can be highly repressed, undeveloped, and ineffectual. Want to create harmony in their environment, to avoid conflicts and tension, to preserve things as they are, to resist whatever would upset or disturb them.)

21. What advice do you have for others who want to make this behavior change or any other?

22. Any other comments?

Appendix B - Consolidating My Learning

Get more out of this book by asking yourself the questions below as you read each story. These questions can also be used as a guide for discussion with your book club, worksite or community support group, family or friends. While all questions may not apply to each story, we provide them here because we have learned that each story can be interpreted differently by each reader.

These questions can serve as a source of reflection as you prepare yourself or someone else for successfully changing a behavior. Record some of your reactions to those stories that you find most compelling. A form on which to record your thoughts as the stories and questions compel you is provided below. Note that for those of you who might wish to keep this form on your personal computer or your Personal Digital Assistant (PDA), go to www.healthimprovementsolutions.com, click the "Resources" link, click on How and Why People Change Health Behaviors, and then click on "Behavior Change Planning Log," to download this document.

Here are the questions we suggest you ask yourself as you read each story:

How This Story Relates to Me

1. What do I think are the most motivational aspects from this story for me?
2. Can I derive any motivation from this story for my own situation?
3. Do I have some things in common with this changer?
4. What was the most interesting part of this story for me?
5. What was the most surprising part of this story for me?
6. Is this story a good model for me in establishing personal goals?
7. What are my similarities and differences with this changer?

My Key Learning Points

1. What are the key learning points from this story for me?
2. During what part of the story did I feel like the changer finally made the total commitment necessary to make behavior change(s)? What can I learn from this?
3. Do I see the importance of taking small steps that lead to lasting change from this story?
4. Did this story help me put relapse and overcoming it into perspective?
5. Changing two behaviors at once can be too difficult. What did I learn by hearing how this person addressed and successfully changed more than one behavior?
6. Does this story help me understand the importance of rewards?
7. What are the main tips and strategies that I learned from this story?

My Action Steps

1. What was this changers support structure? How will I develop a support structure for making my behavior changes?
2. What did I learn by reading about this person's planning behaviors and what is my plan for change?
3. What environmental changes did this changer make and what environmental changes will I need to make to be successful?
4. What are some small steps I can take now that will help me reach lasting behavior change?
5. How might I reward myself for making a successful behavior change?
6. Am I prepared for relapse? How will I deal with it if it does occur?

In using the form that follows, choose those stories that compel you (even if it is all of them) and then answer the questions above for each. Note that the questions were broken into three categories. Those same three categories are found on the form. Write brief responses to each question, or groups of questions on the form. Then use the information to set specific action steps you can follow to make appropriate change. Note that an example if provided to give you ideas on how to get started.

Sample

The Changer	Page No.	How This Story Relates To Me	My Key Learning Points	My Action Steps
Maureen G.	8	**My Answers:** My age is similar to Maureen's and I am female too. I am overweight and don't eat right. We both grew up in one of those "clean your plate" households. I have sometimes suffered from depression, just like Maureen. I was very surprised that she made her changes by taking small steps and she did it without professional help! She lost 80-90 pounds — that is very motivational to me! Maureen is a single parent and so am I. Her changes have made her feel happier and her children are proud of her. I can't wait to get going!	**My Answers:** A key learning is that if you can do something for 30 days, you can do it for a lifetime. I never thought of it like that before. Maureen seemed to really turn the corner when she started to get up early to exercise. This also helped her avoid embarrassment. I am not sure how Maureen avoided relapse, but I think I can learn more from other stories. Maureen was able to loose weight by starting with exercise. That made her more nutrition conscious, which led to weight loss. Maureen got rewards from a worksite program. I am probably going to have to find a different way. **Change Ideas:** • Get good shoes for walking • Change your exercise routine so you don't get bored • Do exercise routines you enjoy • Spend sometime on yourself	**My Action Steps:** • Find someone to walk with • Ask my children for their support • Plan exercise into my day • Learn more about nutrition • Limit un-healthy food in the house • Buy new walking shoes • Plan meals in advance • For every 10 pounds I loose I am going to take the kids on a long weekend to a state park lodge (where we will have fun but get plenty of exercise) • If I relapse I am going to reflect for one day, and then get back on the horse and ride • I am going to loose 50 pounds, eat healthy and be fit • They don't know it but I am going to enter our whole family in the 5K Breast Cancer run this fall (and I am going to beat the kids!)

My Planning Log

The Changer	Page No.	How This Story Relates To Me	My Key Learning Points	My Action Steps
		My Answers:	**My Answers:** **Change Ideas:**	**My Action Steps:**
		My Answers:	**My Answers:**	**My Action Steps:**

My Planning Log

The Changer	Page No.	How This Story Relates To Me	My Key Learning Points	My Action Steps
		My Answers:	**My Answers:** **Change Ideas:**	**My Action Steps:**
		My Answers:	**My Answers:**	**My Action Steps:**

My Planning Log

The Changer	Page No.	How This Story Relates To Me	My Key Learning Points	My Action Steps
		My Answers:	**My Answers:** **Change Ideas:**	**My Action Steps:**
		My Answers:	**My Answers:**	**My Action Steps:**

Appendix C — References

Comments by interviewees on any products or programs should not be viewed as an endorsement by the book or its authors. In an effort to allow each interviewee to tell his or her own story, all statements made were left unchanged. The mention of specific products or programs just demonstrates the variety of solutions that people have used to help them be successful. So that you know where to find any products and programs mentioned, we have provided contact information below.

101 Ways to Lose Weight
Rodale, Inc.
33 East Minor Street
Emmaus, PA 18098-0099
(610) 967-5171
www.rodale.com

American Heart Association
American Heart Association
National Center
7272 Greenville Avenue
Dallas, TX 75231
800-AHA-USA-1
www.americanheart.org

The American Stroke Association
American Stroke Association
National Center
7272 Greenville Avenue
Dallas, TX 75231
888-4-STROKE
http://www.strokeassociation.org

Body for Life
EAS, Inc.
555 Corporate Circle
Golden, CO 80401
800-297-9776
http://www.bodyforlife.com

Corporate Cup
http://www.omahacorporatecuprun.org

Curves
Curves International
100 Ritchie Road
Waco, TX 76712
800-848-1096
http://www.curvesinternational.com

Dump Your Plump
(269) 925-3524
Toll free: (800) 67PLUMP
Email: info@dumpyourplump.com
http://www.dumpyourplump.com

The Food Guide Pyramid
Center for Nutrition Policy and Promotion
3101 Park Center Drive
Room 1034
Alexandria, VA 22302-1594
(703) 305-760
http://www.cnpp.usda.gov

Jenny Craig
Jenny Craig International
5770 Fleet Street
Carlsbad, CA 92008
(760) 696-4000
http://www.jennycraig.com

Kathy Smith
Note that there are many Kathy Smith Videos and Books advertised on the Internet. Below is information for videos.
Workout Music Video
PO Box 2730
Alpharetta, GA 30023
(770) 664-1375
http://www.workoutmusicvideo.com

Nautilus
1400 NE 136th Avenue
Vancouver, Washington 98684
800-782-4799
http://www.nautilus.com

Nutrition-For-You
SciMedica, The Source of Natural Medicine.
501 Faulconer Drive
Suite 2C
Charlottesville, Virginia 22903-4980
(804) 293-6446
http://www.nutritionforyou.com

Prevention Magazine
Rodale, Inc.
33 East Minor Street
Emmaus, PA 18098-0099
(610) 967-5171
http://www.prevention.com

Weigh Down Workshop
The Weigh Down Workshop
PO Box 689099
Franklin, TN 37068-9099
888-829-7500
http://www.wdworkshop.com

Weight No More, Inc.
888-868-3663
http://www.weightnomoreinc.com

Weight Watchers
Columbus Circle Station
PO Box 21053
New York, NY 10023
Available http://www.weightwatchers.com

Weight Watchers Corporate Solutions
800-8-AT-WORK (800-828-9675)
http://www.weightwatchers.com/about/cpp/index.aspx

99630214R00122

Made in the USA
Columbia, SC
10 July 2018